THROUGH THE MOUNTAINS
VALLEYS AND GLOOM...

But Never Alone!

A memoir
by

BARRY FORREST MALAC

Through the Mountains, Valleys and Gloom...
But Never Alone

Copyright © 2008

Barry F. Malac

ISBN: 978-1-880726-24-2

Published by:
Turnage Publishing Co., Inc.
6737 Low Gap Road
Blairsville, GA 30512
(706) 745-5125   sturnage@alltel.net

Printed in the United States by Morris Publishing
3212 East Highway 30
Kearney, NE 68847
1-800-650-7888

"There are only two ways to live one's life:
one is to live as if everything is a miracle,
the other one is as if nothing is a miracle."

Albert Einstein

FOREWORD

I write this memoir not to boast about my own accomplishments, but rather to witness about the love, mercy and grace of our heavenly Father, who is the giver of life and of everything that is good. The life that God has so graciously given me is an unbelievable miracle. I have no other intellectually rational explanation of the events that have shaped my entire life.

First and foremost, I believe that "all things work together for good to them that love God" (Rom. 8:28). It is God's grace and the power of the Holy Spirit that has brought me this far. These miracles in my life are nothing but lucky coincidences to most unbelievers, but to me they represent God's fulfillment of his promises to those who put their trust in Him.

The other reason for sharing my life story is to let my children and grandchildren know and understand that is it not just my life that has been so richly blessed, but their lives as well. Our accomplishments are not ours alone. We build and stand on the shoulders of all generations that have preceded us. You can be justly proud and grateful for the generations of Christian ancestors reaching back across the centuries of time. They were some of the early beneficiaries of the work of two Greek brothers, Cyril and Methodius, who brought the Gospel to my Slavic fore-fathers in the tenth century, and who gave them the Holy Scriptures in their native language.

They were the forerunners of the Moravian faith. Later, the early Moravians suffered for centuries for their faith. Many were persecuted, and even died for their faith. Thousands left their native land to find refuge in a strange land and an opportunity to worship in freedom according to their belief.

So it was even with my generation. We too were denied the right to worship according to the dictates of our heart. My wife and I were faced with a choice: either stay put and suffer in silence under the pressure of a godless political regime, or leave the land of my forefathers, leave family and friends and go to our "promised land," where our children and their children could grow up free to chose their own way of life, hopefully a life anchored by belief in God.

This memoir would not have seen the light of day had it not been for the patiently persistent urging of my dear wife, Marian. I am deeply grateful for her inspiration, her help in typing and re-typing this story over and over from my handwritten pages to bring this effort to fruition.

I am particularly thankful for the perceptive and sensitive review of my manuscript by Mrs. Arlene Gray of Blairsville who is an accomplished, published author, and above all, one of God's angels in her own right. I am grateful for her suggested title for the book. I have been struggling for months to come up with a catchy title without success. She has also offered a ringing endorsement of my meager effort, which you can read on the back cover.

I dedicate this memoir to our children and grandchildren. I hope they will catch a glimpse of this wonderful miracle that God has performed in my life. It is my ardent prayer that all who read this story will be inspired to dedicate their lives to God and to His service.

PROLOGUE

My ancestral home, the small village of Herspice tucked away in the southeastern corner of Moravia, was in more recent history a part of the great Austro-Hungarian Empire. While the village itself might not posses a great deal of natural appeal, it has much to offer in the realm of history.

For one thing, it has been around since the 13th century according to the earliest written records. It was then a part of a Slavkov barony in the possession of King Vaclav IV. Later in 1422 it became the property of Sigismund, the Emperor of the Holy Roman Empire. In 1507 the Slavkov estate, including Herspice village, became a possession of the prominent Kounic family and remained so until the end of World War I.

Perhaps the most historically significant event that took place in Herspice and on the entire Slavkov estate, was the famous battle of the Three Emperors in 1805. On their march to Russia, the French armies flooded the entire region, ransacking and pillaging all settlements in their way. Local historians tell of the French soldiers eating everything in sight in the village of Herspice except for one fatted goose, which a farmer's wife hid in a large hollow willow tree.

To halt the march of the invaders, the Austrian Emperor Franz I and Russian Emperor Alexander II joined forces and met Napoleon's army on the famous battlefield near Austerlitz. The French soundly defeated the Austrians and Russians, and the three emperors met at one house in Herspice, house number 45, to sign the articles of a peace treaty.

Another significant, although rather unknown historical fact, is that it was here in Herspice, in the Czech Brethren Church, on August 31, 1880, that Thomas Garrigue Masaryk joined the Evangelical Church of Czech Brethren. He is the same man who later became the first president of the new Czechoslovak Republic at the end of World War I.

My family history does not go nearly as far into the past as the history of the village. All I know is that during the early 1800's my great-grandfather Josef and his wife Marie appear on the scene. Josef was a "chalupnik" (chalupa means a cabin). That meant that he was given a small house and a plot of land by the estate owner, on which he could grow some produce for his family. As was the custom in those days, he and his wife raised a large family that provided the necessary labor force to grow his crops and raise some livestock.

Their son Josef, born in 1858, who became my grandfather, was probably the first child, since he was named after his father. His wife, my grandmother, was Jenovefa (Genevieve) nee Hrabovska. These paternal grandparents are the only ones I knew, and the ones I can remember.

My grandfather and grandmother owned a country store and bakery, and my grandfather served as the mayor of the village. They raised 14 children, ten boys and four girls, twelve of whom lived to adulthood. The family belonged to the Protestant Reformed church.

My father, Gustav Josef, was born in 1881 as the fourth child. As a young boy, he was sent to Prague to be an apprentice in a large grocery store. After finishing his apprenticeship, he went to live with his aunt in Berlin, in order to improve his German language.

There he came in contact with the young people of the Methodist Church. Their enthusiasm for God's work brought him to feel the need for a deeper spiritual life, and it was there in Berlin that he gave his life to Christ. In 1909 he was received into the membership of the Methodist Church. When he felt the call into the ministry, he was sent to study at the Seminary in Frankfurt on the Mainz. At the same time, he was assigned to preach in the Fourth Methodist Church in Berlin.

When the First World War broke out, the Seminary was closed and the teachers and students were drafted into the army. By that time, my father was preaching for a short time in Backa, Slovenia and later in the small Czech Methodist Church in Vienna, Austria. But he was also drafted into the Austrian army, and after training, was sent to the front lines. After the war, he became a fulltime pastor of the Czech congregation in Vienna, in February 1920. It was there that my life began.

Chapter
1
The Time Between the Wars

A momentous event occurred in Vienna on December 12, 1923, I was born. I became part of the Methodist parsonage of Gustav Josef Malac and Antonie Malacova, as their third child. The first was a girl who died before she was two years old, and she was followed by the birth of my brother Vlastislav in 1921. Rounding out our family two years after my birth, Jirina, my sister, was born. Three children close in age can get into some interesting situations, and that was certainly true of the three of us, especially of us two boys.

There is not much that I remember about Vienna in those early years, although I lived there until I was five. The parsonage was located in a fairly new subdivision called "Siedlung Eden," meaning paradise. Our subdivision was a part of the Viennese suburb Huttledorf, and the parsonage stood on a street quaintly named Knodlehuttenstrasse. The house was a brick and stone structure with a basement and two floors, built by my father with help from his brothers. Behind the house was a large garden where my father used to grow a lot of vegetables and fruits. Across the street from the house was a large meadow, and beyond it more meadows and woods stretched up the hill. During the summertime, neighborhood children could be seen grazing their ducks, geese, goats and sheep there. All of it was quite a bucolic setting.

I recall that in the winter, we would be sledding down our street, sloping down to a small stone bridge across a small stream. Sometimes we did not quite reach the bridge, and my brother and I would end up in that creek. In the spring we would take our flock of ducks and geese to the meadow to graze. We even had one goat that my mother kept, in order to have milk for us children.

On Sundays we would take a train into the city to my father's church. In the afternoon we would go on walks with the whole family, visit with friends, or have a picnic lunch. Sometimes we would walk down the street into the village of Huttledorf and visit the Schoennbrun palace and its beautiful gardens.

The summers were spent mostly with my paternal grandparents in Herspice. Some of the most memorable times I recall were spent in my grandfather's store. There on the counter stood a large sugar cone from which my grandfather would chip off the amount of sugar that a customer would ask for. According to my grandfather, the sweetest part of the sugar cone was the very tip of the cone. Every time he would put a new sugar cone on the counter, we would ask for the tip of the cone to eat as candy. And oh, how sweet it was!

Every Saturday was a big day for us kids, it was bread baking day. People from the entire village would bring their huge round loaves of bread to the bakery to be baked. My grandfather would lay a large fire into the huge brick oven and would keep it going all through the night. Then early in the morning he would sweep the oven clean, and would start putting the bread in the oven with a long-handled wooden paddle. There must have been over fifty round loaves of bread, each about 18 inches in diameter. I remember that the whole floor of the baking room would be covered with the loaves of bread in their straw baskets, so that there was hardly any room to walk. My brother, Vlastik, and I would come to watch, and our grandfather would try to shoo us out with the long wooden paddle. But once the bread started baking, what a heavenly aroma!

Our favorite treat on Saturday was to get a thick slice of the still hot bread, preferably the "patka" or heel. Then we would take the slice of bread to grandma, who smeared it generously with goose lard. Then the piece de resistance! We would go to the store where grandpa had a wooden barrel of denatured granular salt (cattle saltlick, really), and "plop" went the slice of bread with the greased side down into the salt barrel. Curled up on top of the large brick oven, where it was cozy and warm, we would enjoy our freshly baked bread with grandma's goose lard and with grandad's salt lick. I doubt that even Olympian ambrosia could hold a candle to our delicious slice of grandad's bread.

Next to our grandad's store was the village smithy, where my brother and I would watch the blacksmith make horseshoes, shoe the horses, put iron bands on wooden wheels, and do all sorts of things with a piece of white hot iron, hammer, and an anvil. It was fascinating to hear the clang of the hammer on the anvil, to smell the steam from the hot iron thrust in a barrel of cold water. To us that was entertainment plus. Those summers we spent in Herspice were really the only time we saw our grandfather and grandmother and their family. When we finally moved from Vienna, we never again saw our grandparents. Both of them passed away a few years after that.

I never knew my maternal grandparents, at least I do not recall ever meeting them. There were eight children in my mother's family, six girls and two boys. I remember all of the aunts, but I never met the two uncles.

The Methodist Episcopal Church South established a mission in Czechoslovakia in 1920. At first it was part of relief work in collaboration with the American Red Cross and other charitable agencies, but soon it became evident that there was a great need for spiritual revival as well.

Seeing the opportunity to serve as a Methodist minister in his native country, and since we children were reaching school age, father requested a transfer from the Austrian Conference to the Czechoslovak Conference of the Methodist Episcopal Church South. On January 1, 1929 he became the pastor of the congregation in Bratislava, Slovakia.

The only thing I remember quite vividly about living in Bratislava was the hard winter we had early in 1929. There was so much snow, that the people had to dig tunnels through the deep snowdrifts to get to their houses. Our stay in Bratislava was short. By the summer of 1929, we moved to a large church in Pilsen in western Bohemia.

In Pilsen we found our first "real" church. The missionary support from the Methodist Church made it possible to build a beautiful new and modern church building with a steeple and an attached parsonage. The church even had a full time janitor who lived in the basement apartment of the parsonage. This was heaven to us kids, because so far, everywhere we had lived previously, we had to commute to the church. Here we were living right next to the church, separated from the parsonage only by a covered passageway.

That year it was time for me to start school. The elementary school was just a few city blocks away, down the street from the parsonage. My mother took me the first day. I had a brand new satchel, a nice slate, and an abacus. But, for some unexplainable reason, my mother gave my teacher a switch to use on me if I misbehaved. I could not believe that she would do something like that to a sweet little boy, just starting out on his educational journey. Of course, I had let it slip out more than once that I would "bust up" the classroom. But, as it turned out, I liked school, and did very well, even though the teacher dusted my pants with that switch quite frequently. Life settled into a routine.

One summer when I was in the second or third grade, our parents were gone to Prague to the Annual Conference of the Church, and we were left home alone for about three days. The sexton's wife living in the basement apartment would cook for us, and generally kept an eye on us. But one afternoon, my brother and I decided to climb to the top of the church steeple. The steeple was a square structure, rising about 25 feet above the roof of the sanctuary, with a flat top and a lightning rod on top. Fire escape ladders went up the side of the building to the flat roof of the sanctuary, and then on to the top of the steeple. As we reached about the midpoint of the steeple, we saw our five-year-old sister climbing the ladder to the sanctuary roof. She just wanted to join us, she said. All three of us scaled the tower and stood around the lightning rod, enjoying the view below, and feeling we had conquered Mt. Everest. Soon we spotted a bunch of people standing around on the street below, looking up and pointing to the sky, and a police car speeding down the street. It did not take long before two policemen appeared on top of the steeple and wanted to know who we were and what we were doing on top of the tower. Needless to say, the incident caused quite a stir in the congregation and the neighborhood. But we had our day in the sun.

After completing elementary school, I went to the "gymnasium" or high school, which was located right across the street from the parsonage. As it turned out, it was very convenient for me. One of the required classes was religion. Since most of the students in the school were Catholics, the priest would come and teach catechism right there in our classroom. Those of us who were not Catholic were excused, and had a free hour. There were about four or five of us non-Catholics who had one free hour every week. One of the students was a Jewish boy, Franz Lewit. During our free hour, he and I went over to the parsonage for a snack and to do whatever boys do. We became close friends. He introduced me to the Boy Scouts and even invited me to his Bar Mitzvah.

The early 1930's were hard years. The big depression in America was felt even in Czechoslovakia. The missionary support dwindled, as America had to tighten its collective belt. The Methodist Church had to cut salaries of all ministers by fifty percent. The bishop advised the ministers to take on other jobs to supplement their income. Over half of the Methodist preachers in Czechoslovakia left the ministry. My father was one of those who chose to stay with his congregation.

The political climate in all of Europe became rather gloomy and uncertain. In Austria, Hitler took advantage of the economic uncertainties to start up his political campaign of National Socialism by promising Germans he would seek reparations for the injustice of the Treaty of Versailles. At home, there was talk of the communist party being the promise of a bright economic future, and there was fear of a new war with Germany. By 1936, Italy invaded Ethiopia, the Nazis took the Saar, the Spanish Civil War had broken out, and in England the English King abdicated his reign to marry an American divorcee. In the midst of all this turmoil, Berlin and Herr Hitler were preparing for the Olympic Games to showcase the power of the "Aryan" race. At least the promise of the Games brought a bit of respite from all the political and social upheaval.

My mother, my brother Vlastik, my sister Jirina, and I were all involved in the national gymnastic and patriotic organization "Sokol" meaning Falcon. As the Olympic torch was making its way from Greece across Europe, some members of the "Sokol" were chosen as torchbearers. My brother and I got to carry the torch for about half a kilometer each in the middle of the night. But there were no TV cameras or reporters then. Well, so much for my moment of glory.

In 1938, all of us took part in the big Sokol gymnastic games in Prague. These national games were also held every four years. All age levels of gymnasts, from 8 to 70 years of age, competed in mass calisthenics, up to 40,000 participants, and in track and field events. It was the last such meet before the World War II erupted in 1939.

We stayed in Pilsen for eight years. This was an unusually long time for a Methodist preacher, but the hard economic times forced the Church to economize by relocating fewer ministers. In 1937, my father was sent to Slany, a small town in central Bohemia, some 25 miles northwest of Prague.

The news of the impending move from Pilsen dealt me a horrific emotional blow. I was then in the third year of the gymnasium, or 8th grade. There was this one beautiful girl with blond curly hair, dimpled cheeks, and the most alluring smile. I was head over heels in love with her, a really classic case of puppy love. Not to see her again was unthinkable for me. But she had plenty of suitors, and she probably did not even know that I existed. I was the shortest kid in the class, including the girls. I was skinny, and wore funny-looking round eyeglasses. Everybody called me "Ghandi". Oh well, as it turned out, I survived.

By the time we moved to Slany, the war hysteria was reaching its peak. The talk of war was everywhere. Hitler had rearmed Germany and began to lay claim to more territories, a new "Lebensraum" for the "superior German race." Inside Germany, several infamous concentration camps were already full of Jews, and other "undesirable elements," as Nazis called them. For some time the Czechoslovak army had been building fortifications along the western borders with Germany and now declared a general mobilization. The government ordered evacuation of young children from the border area, and began placing them with families inland. My mother took one young girl into our family, even though we had very little space in our parsonage.

It seemed that everything was in turmoil; even our family was not spared. My brother, Vlastik, had to move to Prague to attend school. In Pilsen he had attended a technical high school, but there was no such school in Slany. Since a daily commute was out of the question, he had to move to Prague. Fortunately, the Central Methodist Church there had a spare room in the church building, where he could stay. Vlastik came home only for Christmas and during summer vacations. My sister and I were able to continue our studies in Slany.

Even though I had started in a classical high school in Pilsen, there was no problem in transferring to a regular high school, because the first three grades in the classical high school were the same as the regular high school. Having anticipated the move, it worked out just right for me.

In the spring of 1938, Hitler took over Austria and demanded that Czechoslovakia cede the Sudetenlands, those areas bordering Germany, where the predominant population was German, as a result of the three hundred year occupation by the Hapsburg Empire. Sudeten Germans were demonstrating under the leadership of Henlein, a German political activist, demanding union with Germany. Over 20,000 Sudeten Germans fled to Germany, their "Vaterland". Finally in September 1938, the Munich agreement gave in to Hitler's demands, and ordered the Czechoslovak government to give up the Sudetenlands for the sake of world peace. Hitler was appeased again.

Nothing seemed right after that. The nation felt betrayed by our allies and exposed to further demands by Germany, since we were now without the protection of the beautiful mountain ranges in our border lands. The fortifications built along the German borders fell into German hands without a single shot, as a result of the Munich pact. It did not take but about six months more for Hitler to occupy the rest of Czechoslovakia.

That happened around the middle of March 1939. As my sister and I were walking to school that day, we were stopped on the main street by a long, armed convoy of the German army rolling into the center of town. Tanks, heavy artillery pieces, troop carriers were filling up the town. Along the streets, people watched in disbelief and grief. Some were crying, others shaking their fists. Even though I was only 16 years old, I, too, felt a very personal betrayal by our "friends" and western allies, who had promised to come to our aid in case of armed attack.

Our beautiful and proud Czechoslovakia became a Protectorate of the hated Hitler's Third Reich. Everywhere one would see the ugly symbols of Hitler's "Thousand Year Empire", the swastika, the black uniforms of the feared SS troops, and the long, black leather overcoats of the Gestapo Secret Service. And it did not take long before Jewish citizens were required to wear a yellow Star of David on their clothing. Soon after that, Jews, political leaders, and other "undesirable" elements began to disappear into the dreaded concentration camps.

We stayed in Slany only about three more months after the German occupation. In the summer of 1939, my father was appointed to a church in Jihlava, in the southeastern part of Moravia's borderland. We were all understandably apprehensive about our move.

Chapter

2

The World at War

Jihlava was a walled, medieval city, with some parts of the old walls still standing. The church building we were moving into was at one time an elegant patrician villa. It was built sometime around the beginning of the 19th century, just on the south side of the ancient city wall. It stood on the outer bank of the old city moat surrounding the city. The large back yard of the villa was located in the bottom of the moat. It even had an old stone horse stable, with space for a carriage.

The building itself had a full basement with a small apartment for a sexton and his family. The main floor held the sanctuary, created from a couple of large rooms, an office, which served as our living room, and at times as a dining room when we had guests. There was a large kitchen with a spacious, walk-in pantry. A large master bedroom, small bathroom, and a tiny adjacent dressing room, serving as the children's bedroom, completed the living space.

The first problem we faced was the availability of schools. Jihlava had only a classical high school, so I had to commute by train some 20 miles to Havlickuv Brod, the nearest town with the normal high school. Since my sister, Jirina, could not tolerate a train ride without getting sick, the only alternative for her was to go live with our aunt in Uherske Hradiste, in southeastern Moravia. My brother, Vlastik, remained in Prague, to continue his studies in the technical high school. So now our family had shrunk to just three members, my mother, my father, and I, the fortunate one.

On September 1, 1939, my father went with me to Havlickuv Brod to enroll me in the high school there. Since money was tight and we owned two bicycles, we decided to ride the bikes. It was really a beautiful ride. A paved road wound through a lot of woodlands, over hill and dale, and along a winding stream and as I recall, the weather was just beautiful.

Having completed my registration, we started back home shortly after noon. About midway home, we stopped at a dairy store to get a glass of cold milk and a roll. While we were eating, we heard an announcement on the radio that Hitler had declared war on Poland, and that his troops were sweeping across the borders against the capital city of Warsaw.

World War II had just started.

Living conditions worsened with the onset of war. Food and other strategic goods were rationed and everyone was issued coupons for purchasing the same. Especially hard to get, were meat and dairy products because most of the agricultural products went to Germany for the support of its fighting armies. To improve our food situation, we raised geese, ducks, chickens and rabbits. To secure grain for feed, Vlastik and I spent summers working on farms to help with the harvest of crops. For payment we asked for grain and meat.

That first summer, my brother and I went to work on a state farm in Mysliborice, about 30 miles away, where our uncle was an overseer. Our job was to take care of feeding 40 milking cows, 60 pigs, and eight teams of draft horses. Besides that, we signed up along with about 20 or 30 other field hands, to work for a week in the field hoeing several hectares of sugar beets.

The work was not too bad, although the hours were long, usually from sunup to sundown. But the food was excellent, because we stayed with our Uncle Josef and his wife Ruzena (Rosie), who was an excellent cook. On weekends we would listen to our uncle play his accordion and listen to stories about rural life under the German occupation, which was not easy. All farms, state and private, had to report their crop yields and meat and dairy production, and bring ten percent of all products to a collection center to be shipped to Germany.

My uncle told us about a large hog that he was raising on the sly, so that he would not have to report it to the authorities. The hog was already close to 600 pounds, when he decided to slaughter it. To keep the hog out of view, he kept it in a small covered sty. He planned to kill the hog in the middle of the night. Usually, to kill a hog, he would shoot it in the head. Afraid of waking up the whole neighborhood with a gunshot, he decided to stun the beast with a blow to the head with an axe and then slit its throat with a knife. Having very little room in the crowded hog pen to swing an axe, he straddled the hog between his legs and delivered a blow to the head. The hog jerked to get loose, the axe missed the head, and struck the poor critter in the eye. The squeals and the frantic thrashing of the huge beast in the tight confines of a pig sty created a racket louder than any sound of a gunshot. Pretty soon most of the farm and a good part of the village populace were aware of what was going on. But of course, my uncle said, he always intended to share his good fortune with his "good German masters."

With Germany at war, the political conditions at home worsened as well. The Gestapo was conducting searches, arresting people for infractions of curfews and all sorts of other violations of the new German laws for occupied lands. In schools, all subjects now had to be taught in German. History was not taught at all, as all history books were confiscated, and new history books were being prepared by the German government. Things were slowly going from bad to worse. In less than two years since the start of the war, Hitler's armies occupied all of Europe, northern Africa, and were on the move to Russia.

It was at this point of my life that my path had crossed with another young man, Vaclav Bedrnik, or Vasek, as he was called. He, too, moved to Jihlava that year from the Sudetenland in the northwestern part of Bohemia after the German occupation. The two of us were the only two students commuting from Jihlava to Havlickuv Brod high school, and fate had placed us into the same class.

Soon Vasek and I became very close friends. Vasek was one of those people mature well beyond his years. He was a natural leader, he spoke fluent German, he spoke well, he was self-assured, he knew what he wanted in life. He was outgoing and made friends easily. I found myself dominated by his personality. The two of us became known as inseparable, and rather notorious throughout the high school. We became the "leaders" in our class; where there was mischief, we were at the heart of it. But we were simply reacting to the oppressive atmosphere of the German occupation. School was no fun any more. Every morning we had to sing the German national anthem, "Deutchland Uber Alles", and the hated SS song, "Die Fahne Hoch".

Vasek and I enjoyed singing; he played a mandolin and I strummed a guitar. At times, when everyone in the class would feel depressed, we would start singing a jazzed up version of the two hated songs. On several occasions the loud singing would bring a frightened principal to the classroom, threatening to expel the whole lot of us. I am sure that his fear was real, because defamation of the German national anthem was more than enough reason to displease the Gestapo.

But it was not until our senior year that Vasek and I reached the peak of our notoriety. It was the "Big Scrap Metal Caper" that really secured our position as the most talked-about pair. Germany was in a war on many fronts, and strategic supplies, such as metals, were in high demand. Our school was given a quota of scrap metal that needed to be collected by a certain date. Students struggled to bring tin cans and all kinds of metal scraps, trying to reach our goal, but with little success. That's when Vasek and I decided to step in and help the school out.

As mentioned earlier, our parsonage in Jihlava had an old horse stable and a carriage house on the premises. Vasek and I decided that with our parents' permission we would take out the old, cast-iron feed troughs and other cast-iron fixtures from the stable. We borrowed a small, wooden wagon and loaded it with about half a ton of scrap iron. Then we pulled the wagon to the school, some 20 miles away. In order to arrive at the school at mid-morning for the greatest impact, we left in the evening of the day before. Making pretty good progress, we reached the outskirts of Havlickuv Brod shortly after midnight. We looked for a place to rest and to wait until morning. Soon we spotted a large haystack, not far from the road, so we pulled up to the stack, buried ourselves into the hay, and went to sleep.

After sunup, we took off and headed for the school. As we were approaching the school, some of our classmates spotted us from a second story window, as we pushed the wagon uphill toward the school. Before too long, what looked like the whole student body, including the teachers and the principal, were spilling out of the building, waving their arms, yelling, and generally creating quite a ruckus. Precisely what we wanted to achieve: maximum impact!

The principal, though, did not seem to appreciate our efforts on behalf of the Third Reich. But our fame became secured. As a matter of fact, years later when I was able to attend my 40th class reunion, my homeroom teacher, who was still living, reminded me of that incident. He said he did not remember much of anything else about me, except that.

My favorite teacher was Dr. Kabrda our French teacher. He had studied at the Sorbonne University in Paris, spoke fluent French and Arabic. He always encouraged his students to learn as many foreign languages as possible, and also to learn at least one exotic language. "You never know when it might become useful to you," he would say.

Besides being an accomplished linguist, he was also an excellent musician and a lover of theater and dramatic arts. He inspired our class to put on plays and literary recitals.

I was always interested in theatrical arts, and so I participated in several plays. Vasek, on the other hand, was not interested in acting. His passion was writing and poetry. But we both participated in the cast parties after the performance. Our specialty was to provide escort for all the girls on their way home after the party, and to serenade each of the girls at the door. It was a somewhat risky undertaking, since there was a 10 o'clock curfew. But somehow we had escaped discovery by the police and the Gestapo, until after our school senior play. We then decided not only to escort the girls home, but to continue with the party all night, and stay away from school the next day. The party was held at a remote location in a summer home belonging to the uncle of one of our class members.

Quite obviously, the whole school was in turmoil when most of one of the senior classes did not show up the next day. The principal was beside himself with fear of the Gestapo, especially since one of the truants was his own son. There were lots of frantic phone calls from parents looking for missing children, calls from police, and even the Gestapo. I remember that even my sister came to Havlickuv Brod to investigate my whereabouts. I don't exactly remember how things finally got sorted out, but one thing I know for sure. Things were not the same after that.

Soon after the ill-fated party, the worst fears of our frazzled principal materialized. The Germans decided to close our school, and conscripted about a dozen of us for work in Germany. I suspect that the principal may have had a hand in the fact that Vasek and I were among those selected to work in Germany to support the German war effort. This was a rather common occurrence all over Europe. All countries occupied by Germany were forced to supply workers for Germany's industries, because Germany's own laborers were then engaged in the war in all of Europe and Africa.

We had no idea what our destination would be. But on March 21, 1943, we boarded a train bound for Prague, where we were to meet with other conscripts from all over the Czech-Moravian Protectorate and be transported on a special train to Germany. There, we finally found out that the train was bound for Munich, in southern Germany. We pulled out of the Wilson Station in Prague around nine o'clock that night. Since ours was a special train, we were stopped in many stations to allow regularly scheduled trains or special troop trains to pass. It was a long and grueling trip; it took us almost two days and two nights to arrive in Munich. Passing through Nurenberg, we saw the first real evidence of the war. Nurenberg was bombed just a week before by the British Royal Airforce.

We arrived in Munich about midnight of the third day. There, we were ordered off the train, and were marched under heavy guard to the famous Hofbrauhaus brewery. Expecting our first real meal in two days, we were disappointed, when instead of feeding us, the guard led us down into the huge underground cellar, where we spent the night among the huge barrels of beer without a bite to eat or drink. It was a cold and miserable night.

Apparently, Munich was one of the main processing centers where hundreds of thousands of conscripts from all of Europe were brought, in order to be assigned to various labor camps throughout Germany. In the morning, Vasek and I, and about 4 or 5 of our other classmates, were assigned to a group of around 40 people, and marched back to the rail station. The guards told us that our group was going to a camp in Erding, some 25 miles northeast of Munich. Finally, we at least knew where we were going, but still did not know anything about the town, the camp, or the kind of work we would be assigned to do.

The trip to Erding took only about one hour. When we got off the train, we were marched along the railroad track for about a mile or two, to a "Stalag" with a high barbed wire fence, and armed guards at the gate. There were several rows of wooden, military style barracks, a large mess hall, latrines, and other storage buildings. And there were deep trenches running in zig-zag fashion between and around the barracks. They looked much like World War I trenches. Much later, as I watched my favorite TV serial, "Hogan's Heroes", I would remember the days in our "Stalag", which, I think, could have served as a model for the TV show. Why, we even had our own "Colonel Klink" and the amiable "Sargeant Schultz". Thus began one of the most memorable parts of my life.

Chapter
3

Stalag Erding

The town of Erding was a typical Bavarian town. It was some 25 miles northeast of Munich, the capital of Bavaria, a province of Germany. The surrounding countryside was a pastoral scene of green fields, meadows and small plots of woodlands. Looking at the peaceful countryside, the war seemed worlds away. That was, at least, until we saw the high barbed wire fence enclosing the Stalag. It was quite a shock to us. We were told we would be living and working together with German workers, and now this? Barbed wire, and a gate with armed guards?

The Stalag was part of a large tactical airbase supporting the Africa Corps of the German army under the command of General Kesselering. The barracks had been used by the pilots of the German Luftwaffe before new facilities were built for them on the airbase itself. Apparently we were to do some kind of work on the airbase.

There were about six or eight wooden barracks, each with ten rooms. A long hallway ran the length of the building with five rooms on each side. In each room were five double bunks with a small locker next to each bunk. On one side of the room was a pot-bellied iron stove. A long table with ten chairs in the middle of the room completed the spartan décor. There were no bathrooms, no running water, the matresses were plain, burlap pallets stuffed with straw. The walls were ordinary, low-grade masonite. Each room had a couple of windows, and one electric lamp hanging from the ceiling in the middle of the room.

Besides the barracks, the camp had a guardhouse by the gate, and a large mess hall with a kitchen. Every two barracks had a separate communal latrine and showers. There was also a small, separate enclosure for some 20 to 25 Russian POW's.

To our pleasant surprise, we found out that there were already a number of Czech conscripts housed in the Stalag. Several of them, in fact, were from around the southeastern and central part of Bohemia. One young man, about my age, was actually from Jihlava where I was from. And even more surprising was the fact that he was a member of my church, a member of our MYF group, and a member of the mandolin band that my father had started and directed.

The entire camp held about 600 workers. Besides the largest contingent of Czechs, there were Frenchmen, Belgians, Poles, and Ukrainians. As we found out later, we were quite fortunate to have landed in such a small camp. Most other labor camps held tens of thousands of workers, and their living conditions were deplorable, to say the least, and far worse than ours.

Once we were assigned to our barracks and room, had stuffed our pallets with straw and settled in, we held our first strategic conference to decide what to do about the barbed wire fence and the armed guards at the gate. Even though we had no idea what our work would be or where we would be working, we decided that we would not leave the Stalag until the armed guards and the barbed wire fence were removed, and that we would demand free access in and out of the Stalag.

The next morning, after breakfast at the mess hall, a group of the new arrivals including Vasek and me, walked out to the gate and sat down. Pretty soon a good many of the old residents of the camp joined us, once they found out what we were about. Our "Sargeant Schulz" came out of the guardhouse to find out what was going on. Our reps told them our demands. Flustered, the sarge ran back to the office and called the airbase Commandant (our "Colonel Klink"), telling him about the strike.

"Get rid of the guards and get these people on the base, at once! They are already late for work! And that's an order!" said the Commandant.

And I am sure God must have smiled. We had won the first round! So we marched, perhaps a quarter-mile or so, to the main hangar of the airbase to report for work to be assigned to our work stations.

The main function of the airbase was aircraft maintenance, to receive new aircraft, equip them with armaments, and have them flown to the front in Africa. The base comprised a total of six hangars, each with specialty shops, a control tower, and the gunnery range. Next to the entrance stood a guardhouse, farther in were the new barracks for the pilots, the commandant, the officers' mess, and a number of warehouses and affiliated workshops. I was properly impressed, since this was the first military airbase I had ever seen.

We walked into the main hangar, where, on the second floor, were the offices for the technical and administrative personnel. The main bay of the hangar was large enough to hold up to six fighter planes, or two small twin engine bombers. Surrounding the main bay were various shops such as the engine room, parts department, machine shop, and a paint shop. Vasek and I were assigned to the engine room. The rest of our group was sent to various shops, like the paint shop, electrical maintenance, various storerooms, etc. I was assigned to an older mechanic named Herre, Herr Herre. He was a little shrimp of a fellow, but kind and understanding, and was very much surprised that I "volunteered" to come to Germany to support the German war effort, the "Drang nach Osten!" After I explained to him that I did not volunteer, but rather that I was conscripted after my high school was closed, he could not believe it. Apparently a lot of people in Germany did not know what was going on in the countries occupied by the German armies. He felt quite embarrassed about the situation. And I found out that many other Germans there were not at all sympathetic to the German expansionary policies.

Just like that, I became an airplane engine mechanic, although I had never seen the inside of any kind of engine, let alone the highly sophisticated engines of the German Luftwaffe.

We were issued work overalls, special shoes with soft soles, and a tool kit with all sorts of wrenches, screw-drivers, pliers, and all kinds of specialized gadgets required for working on the engines. It was interesting, and I almost enjoyed working with my senior mechanic, since I had to make the best of the situation.

And so the routine of being a civilian employee of the Luftwaffe got under way: up in the morning around 5:30 a.m., breakfast at the mess hall, a short walk to the base and my workstation in the engine room. Muster every morning followed on the main floor of the hangar, to make sure that everyone was present and accounted for. Then open the huge hangar doors, and push the planes on the tarmack. After the inspector brought us our work orders, we got to work. Replace sparkplugs, change one doo-dad or another, clean the carburetor, drill a hole here and there, wash the engine block, reseat new valves, replace rings, clean the pistons, all day long! When the inspector came, he checked the work against the work order, and signed the completed work order. That was pretty much the daily routine. The only things that changed from day to day were the airplanes. Throughout those two years I spent at "Mr. Hitler's Resort", I managed to work on just about every war airplane the Luftwaffe used: fighter planes, re-con planes, light bombers, heavy bombers, transport planes, dive bombers, even their newest "secret weapon", the first jet fighters. Things were relatively "peaceful" for us in Germany that first year. German armies were winning on all fronts, their spirits were high so we were even allowed occasionally to eat at the officer's mess hall. After work we could go to eat at local restaurants and visit around town. Vasek and I made some friends among the Germans, and a couple of them invited us to their homes for Sunday dinner.

From time to time, we had to participate in the overnight fire watch. Being on the fire watch meant that a team of about a dozen people had to spend the entire night on the airbase in the firehouse. On one such occasion, I took with me my sketchpad, and after supper I went out, sat on a low hill and began sketching the bucolic countryside. After the daylight began to fade, I started walking back to the firehouse. All of a sudden I found myself facing a couple of grinning Doberman dogs and their handlers. The guard confiscated my sketchpad and took me to the Commandant. Well, I explained that I was not spying, but that I just enjoyed sketching. They let me go back to the firehouse. Lucky for me, at that time I had no incriminating sketches of the airbase in my book. The routine continued, interrupted from time to time by some significant events, some amusing incidents, and some quite exciting happenings.

One day I was working in the main hangar, doing some minor work on a Focke Wolf fighter plane, while next to me the prop specialist was checking out the prop on a ME-108 fighter. He stood on a short ladder, reaching up to loosen the locks on the prop nosecone to remove it. Unbeknown to him, at the same time an electrician climbed into the cockpit to check out the electrical system. Accidentally he pushed the 20mm cannon trigger located on the joystick. The prop man got his arms around the nose cone of the plane, ready to remove it, when simultaneously the cannon discharged. There he was, holding the cowling, the muzzle of the cannon beside his ear, when the shot was fired. The shot shook the hangar, and ended up in the administrative offices on the second floor of the hangar. The prop man stood frozen on the stepladder, holding the cowling, white as a sheet. Everything went deathly quiet for a few seconds. Then everybody jumped up, pried the prop man off the ladder, and helped the mortified electrician out of the cockpit. The prop man was all right, except that he could not hear from his right ear for months afterward. Fortunately, the stray shot went through the outside wall of the hangar without hitting anyone or any important target. It would have been quite comical, had it not been so scary. Incidentally, the young prop man was one of the people who had had Vasek and me over for dinner one Sunday.

Working outside on the line was what I liked the most. When the weather was nice, it was very pleasant outside. One outside job that I did not enjoy, however, was to start up the ME-108's. One of the fastest fighter planes of the Luftwaffe had to be hand-cranked like an old model-T Ford! Actually, it took two men to crank those planes; one man standing on the wheel and the other on the wing, and then you would crank, and crank, and crank. It was hard, especially if the weather was cold. Crank, crank, and ... contact? Most of the time the engine caught, but then there were times when either the engine was too cold, or the pilot flooded the engine, or just missed the right time to push the starter. It was frustrating enough if you had only one plane to crank, but if there were 20 or 30 planes, all ready to take off, it was downright maddening.

I vividly remember one incident when I was personally involved. It was late one Sunday afternoon, right at quitting time, when they pushed a Focke Wolf fighter plane into the hangar. The inspector came and said the plane needed a 25-hour check before taking off to Italy. And wouldn't you know I got stuck with the job, while everybody else went home.

The 25-hour check isn't that much of a deal. Open the cowl, take out the spark plugs (all 32 of them!) check the plugs, the wires, put plugs back in, and that was pretty much all that was needed. I got the plugs out, checked them and the wires, and started to put the plugs back. And as luck would have it, that last sparkplug just would not stay in. I kept tightening and tightening, and the plug just kept turning. Stripped the thread! Oh, what the heck; he still had 31 other plugs to fly on! I snapped the wire to the plug, closed the cowl and called the inspector. He signed the papers and off went the airplane on the tarmack. The pilot climbed in, revved the engine, and taxied for the take-off spot. I watched as he opened the throttle, the plane gathering speed down the runway, and then, just as the wheels began to lift, it happened! The spark plug fell out, and oil gushed out from under the cowling, covered the entire plane from nose to tail, including the entire cockpit. Luckily, the pilot had enough runway left to bring the plane to a stop, turn it around, and taxi back to the hangar with the cockpit open and his face covered with oil. I was not a bit surprised, that as the plane taxied up to the hangar, everybody started to look for me. But the good Lord stood by me, as the inspector took the blame (he really had no choice) and I was sent back to the Stalag. I was just glad that no one was hurt.

On one other occasion, there was a scramble by a couple of wings of fighter planes (ME-108's) to intercept American bombers flying north to bomb some strategic targets. Since the fighters had a long flight before they would actually engage the bombers, they were fitted with auxiliary fuel tanks, attached to the underbelly of the plane. But because the landing gear on the ME-108 was fairly low, there was very little room between the top of the auxiliary tank and the fuselage. There were no more than about 4 to 5 inches of space.

We had to fill up the auxiliary tanks from mobile tankers. Since there were no gauges on the tank to see how much fuel there was, we used our short-handled screwdrivers as dipsticks to check the level of fuel in the tank. We had to work fast, to get the planes in the air and so, in a hurry, I tried to check the fuel level on the tank I was filling, when the screwdriver slipped out of my hand and right into the tank. So what, I thought, full or not, I closed the cap and started for the next plane. This was such an exciting time for the Luftwaffe; the Commandant ("Colonel Klink") was on the flight line, prancing up and down along the row of planes, proud as a peacock. He saw me drop that screwdriver into the tank. Oh, he was livid, and I got a lecture on the dangers of an errant metal screwdriver loose in a tank full of flammable fuel. Well, I remember that lecture to this day. But just like the real Colonel Klink, the Commandant, deep down, was really a pussycat, and let me off the hook without another word. In the end, we got all the planes in the air, the Commandant was happy. But the rumor was that the fighters never engaged the enemy. They were too late. Chalk up one for the good guys!

Chapter
4
The Lighter Side of the War

The first few months in Erding were pretty quiet. The war was being waged on far-flung fronts, far from the "Vaterland". Work was easy and living conditions not bad, considering the circumstances. At work, every two weeks we got a free weekend. Usually we would go to Munich for a day, and spend the other day in camp.

After we had settled into our barracks, I decided to decorate the wall by my bunk. I got hold of some crayons and sketched a picture of the Karlstein castle on the wall. Karlstein was a popular tourist spot, and I had visited the castle a number of times. I had no picture to use as a model, so I sketched it from memory. Actually, it turned out pretty well. When my roommates saw the picture, they wanted me to draw some picture by every bunk in the room. Each one wanted some favorite picture of their own. They picked either a favorite song or poem, or something to remind them of home. I ended up drawing ten different murals.

I had brought my guitar with me. Actually, it was my father's guitar that he had when he was a soldier in the First World War! Soon, I found that there were other guitar players in our barracks. The fellow from my home church happened to have his mandolin with him, so one thing led to another, and it was not too long before we had a permanent group of players and singers. We started singing just for fun in the evenings. Later, we decided to put on an occasional show for the whole camp. We got permission to use the mess hall, which even had a stage of sorts. We organized and staged several programs for the camp, and even included people of other nationalities. We had a

Belgian whistler, who could whistle classical arias from various operas, we had a Russian balalaika player, who was incredibly good. We put on skits, pantomimes, solo and group singing, and even vaudeville and circus acts. Our group became so popular, that we had local citizens come to our parties, and a good many of the German officers as well. We were even asked by the Commandant to play at his Christmas dinner, which he gave for his officers and their wives.

Later on, we were asked to visit a couple of huge labor camps around Munich, each having well over ten thousand occupants. When we saw the conditions in those camps, we realized how fortunate we were in being in the very, very small camp we had in Erding. I am convinced that God's grace, and my mother's prayers had a lot to do with my being where I was. I did not really appreciate the significance of these circumstances until much later, as I reflected on the events that shaped my life, and began to see God's hand in many of the experiences that I have encountered during my entire life.

At other times, with passes, we would enjoy hiking around the countryside, visiting the beautiful museums in Munich, the wonderful zoo, and occasionally visiting the only Methodist church in Munich. Vasek and I made a couple of weekend trips into the Alps and to Lake Constance on the border of Switzerland. But we were not allowed to go visit at home.

By far the biggest adventure Vasek and I planned was to climb the highest peak in the Bavarian Alps, the Grossglockner (the Big Bell). Just like that! In retrospect, it was a very foolish, and a really dangerous idea. We knew absolutely nothing about mountain climbing, and we had no gear to tackle the ice and the snowfields. After all, the Grossglockner is well over 12,000 feet high, permanently covered in snow, and surrounded by glaciers. So what? We were young, and to us it was a great idea and a great challenge.

We started planning our big adventure shortly after we arrived in Erding. We figured out that we needed a minimum of four days to accomplish our goal. We arranged to work for four weeks without a free weekend, so that we could have a four-day weekend. Then we started to get our gear and supplies together. Vasek managed to borrow some climbing ropes, an ice axe, and a couple of rucksacks from one of the old German alpinists who happened to be working in the paint shop on the base. We bought some food supplies, canned foods mostly, borrowed needed maps, and whatever else we felt we needed.

As it worked out, our big trip fell into the middle of May of 1943. The German alpinist who loaned us the equipment warned us that May was about the worst possible time to be in the mountains, because of the avalanche danger. But our minds were made up, and we were going for it. To give ourselves a little extra time, we decided to leave right after work on Thursday. We traveled by train, going south for about three hours to a little village of Ferleiten, where we spent the night in a beautiful Alpine Inn. It was no problem to get a room, because there was nobody else there but us. And again, the owner of the inn told us about the avalanche danger at this time of the year, and advised us against our plan.

The next morning we struck out on foot for the Grossglockner. The weather was sunny and pleasant. We walked through a beautiful valley, heading south. Ahead of us some 10 to 15 kilometers was the beautiful Grossglockner. At the end of the valley we could see a large snowfield rising up to the crest of a ridge, beyond which lay the dangerous Patcherkoffel glacier at the foot of the Grossglockner. We reached the bottom of the snowfield by late afternoon. There was a small wooden shed in a pasture, where the farmer stored his hay for the winter. We decided to spend the night in the barn and get a fresh start the next morning.

In the morning we started our climb. Soon we reached the snowfield. The snow was deep and wet. We sank up to our waists into the snow. Our packs, each weighing about forty pounds, were heavy and growing heavier with each step. We plodded on. Slowly we were gaining altitude. Then about mid-morning we saw and heard what the innkeeper was talking about, an avalanche! On both sides of the narrowing valley the avalanches were coming down. Just about every ten minutes a new avalanche would slide down into the valley. Fortunately, we were far enough from either side of the slopes where the snow was melting and coming down the slopes. We kept on climbing. But the going was hard and progress was slow. By mid-afternoon we were still only halfway to the top. We decided to go back down to the hay barn, spend the night there and start over the next morning.

Next morning we repacked our packs, leaving all extra clothing and supplies at the barn, and started up the snowfield with much lighter packs. We reached the place from which we had returned the previous day by mid-morning. We were making much better time the second time around. But in the afternoon, the weather began to worsen. By the time we reached the edge of the Patcherkoffel glacier the clouds covered the Gross-glockner, and it started to rain. We could see the large resort hotel to our right, the terminus of the autobahn, and on the left the autobahn was winding down into the valley below. The hotel was closed, and there was no one around that we could see. We found a cave at the edge of the glacier, where we stayed out of the rain for some time, contemplating what to do next. It looked like the weather had moved in; there was nothing we could see but the fog. Finally, we decided that our climb would be impossible the next day or two because of the weather, and our time was running out. We decided to abort the climb.

Consulting our map, we found that the closest place we could reach before dark was the little village of Heiligenblut, about 5 kilometers distant, and lying close to the alpine autobahn. So we struck out for Heiligenblut. Tired, soaking wet, and sunburned from spending the previous day on the sunlit snowfield, we reached our Shangri-la. Heiligenblut is one of the most picturesque alpine villages in the world. There we found kind and lovely people who put us up, fed us, and gave us a warm, clean bed. To this day, I recall how incredibly fortunate we were to survive those last two days. The next morning we took a bus back to Ferleiten, went back to the barn to retrieve the rest of our gear, and then took the train back to Erding. So far as Vasek and I are concerned, the Grossglockner remains unconquered.

And there is an interesting footnote to this episode. Some 20 years later, I was back at the Grossglockner Hotel Resort with a tour of foresters, while attending the International Union of Forest Research Organizations meeting in Vienna, Austria. But this time the weather was absolutely beautiful, the sky was a brilliant blue, the sun was shining, and we could see the majestic Grossglockner in all of its glory. And I remember the driver of our tour bus saying that he had been driving the bus to the Grossglockner for the previous twenty years, but this was the first time he had actually seen the mountain.

It was shortly after our mountain climbing adventure that Vasek and I began talking about escaping to Switzerland. But we could not agree on what to do after we would get there. I wanted to go to England, but Vasek insisted on going to Yugoslavia to join Tito's partisans. I knew that Vasek had strong feelings about socialist ideologies, but somehow I just could not see myself as a part of Tito's strong leaning toward communism. After long, and sometimes bitter arguments, we decided to part company. Vasek did manage to reach Switzerland; it had been confirmed by the Swiss Red Cross after the war was over. But then Vasek had decided to strike out for Yugoslavia and Tito's partisans, against the advice of the Swiss authorities who said it would be a dangerous undertaking. Vasek did leave Switzerland, and no one ever heard of him again. His family's search for him ended there in Switzerland.

I was upset about my split with Vasek, but after a couple of weeks, and lots of prayers, I made peace with my decision to stay and wait for another opportunity to get away. Apparently, God did not want me to leave yet.

Then Rene de Tobel entered my life. He was a young man about my age who stayed in the Belgian compound of the camp with his father. His father was a former officer in the Belgian army. After the fall of Belgium, he and his son, Rene, were conscripted as laborers for the German war machine. They both ended up in Erding.

Rene was a fun guy. He spoke French, and I saw an opportunity to improve my French. Rene and I became close friends. He actually convinced our "Seargent Schultz" to let him move to our Czech compound and take over the bunk vacated by Vasek. So now I had a new bunkmate. Isn't it wonderful how God works out things? Now I not only had a new friend, but a new French tutor. From then on, while we were in the camp, I spoke French with Rene, and while I was at work, I spoke German. Pretty soon I was called upon to serve as a French-German interpreter. Finally my school German and French found some practical application.

When weather permitted, we played volleyball and soccer in our spare time. One of my high school classmates and I became the aces on our volleyball team. He and I actually won the doubles championship in the camp. Our soccer team was challenged to a game by German workers. The Germans were quite confident that they would slaughter the ragtag Czech team. But our guys took them on, and we won!

Chapter
5

War Comes to Erding

We had our first taste of the real war around the first of November 1943. It came in the form of our first air raid.

Around midnight, the sirens went off. That was the first time I had heard the piercing wail of a siren. Obviously, it awakened everybody in the camp. At first we really had no idea what to do, but soon the guards came running through the barracks, waking everybody up and shouting, "Herauss, herauss, alle Menchen 'raus!" "Everybody out!"

We really did not want to go anywhere in the middle of the night, but the guards insisted that we get out and get into the trenches. Finally we all ended up in the trenches about 5 feet deep, looking into the night sky, expecting some planes overhead.

All at once, the sky over Munich, southwest of us, lit up with giant rays of searchlights crisscrossing the skies from horizon to horizon. Then we saw them! Target flares dropped from the planes, looking like miniature Christmas trees, floating down like a fiery waterfall. The sky was so bright that we almost could have read a newspaper. What a fireworks display!

We saw the flash of bombs hitting the ground, and heard the throbbing roar of the airplane engines. Anti-aircraft gunnery opened fire, and we could see hundreds of shells bursting in the night sky. Everybody was just awestruck by the immensity of the firepower and the destruction.

The raid lasted no more than 15 minutes. During that time we saw two of the bombers caught in the crosshairs of several searchlights, and then inevitably, saw the direct hit. The planes exploded in midair and the remains cascaded towards the earth like a huge river of fire. Slowly the flares went out, the searchlights went out one by one, and we heard the sound of the bomber formation fading away. Finally, about one hour after the sirens first sounded the air raid, the sirens came on again, sounding the "all clear" signal. The show was over. For the first time I realized what war was all about. People were dying! Up until then our presence here in Stalag Erding had been just one great adventure for us, but now we knew that even our lives might be in jeopardy. For us this was a harsh reminder that the world was at war!

That air raid was the first attack on Munich carried out by RAF bombers. The next day, for the first time, we saw the signs of concern on the faces of our German co-workers. The war was coming closer! But there were no more air raids on Munich until the spring of 1944.

In the meantime, the war in Africa was heating up for the Germans. We could see German planes coming from Africa, shot up full of holes over the Mediterranean Sea by American fighter planes. Some of the planes had taken 30 or more hits, and still made it all the way to Erding Airbase. After the Allied armies established a foothold in Italy, things began to heat up even for us. With Americans firmly entrenched in Italy, they started bombing sorties into the heartland of Germany, hitting strategic targets like factories, munitions depots, railheads and such.

Now we would hear air raid sirens every day, twice a day, the British coming around midnight and the Americans around noon. It became such a precise schedule, that one could set his watch by the sound of the air raid sirens. During the night we no longer paid any attention to the raids. We just stayed in our bunks and hoped for the best. Even the guards would not bother to come around to take us out to the trenches. The air raid sirens during the day meant only one thing for us: the ever-growing Allied dominance of the skies over Germany and all of Europe.

And so it went pretty much every day until about the middle of April 1944. The day was bright and sunny and comfortably warm. About 11 o'clock the sirens went off, and along with everybody else, I climbed down the scaffold where I had been doing some work on one of the engines of a medium bomber, the Heinkel 111. I lay down on the grass by the airplane and waited for the show to start. Sure enough, the formations came, flew up north, unloaded, and then started back again. But this time on their return flight, the formations were far more dispersed than usual: one small squadron after another, even groups of no more than a half-dozen planes. Finally, when we thought that the last of the planes had come and gone, we saw a small group of about six planes tagging way behind the main formation.

Then something new happened. The lead plane appeared to drop some kind of a smoke signal, or flare. As the flare began arching towards the ground, we picked out a sound like a whooshing fire that was getting louder and louder. I had no idea what was happening, but all at once, as if on command, everyone around me was jumping up and running. Just like lemmings running for the sea, everybody seemed to be running for the nearest fence. That fence was some 200 yards away, on the other side of the hangars, and beyond the gunnery range. It was an 8 foot high chain link fence with barbed wire on top. Behind us, the bombs were falling, 500-pounders and incendiaries. The air was full of shrapnel, smoke and fire everywhere! Bedlam! To this day I don't know how I made it to the fence and over it without missing a step. As soon as I cleared the fence, I jumped into a ditch by the dirt road that ran alongside that fence. The last bombs hit the ground all around me at the same time that I hit the dirt.

At once a deathly silence! I shook off some debris and dirt off my back, and sneaked a peak to see what was happening. People around me began to pop up like prairie dogs, looking dazed, but seemingly unhurt. On the airfield, hangars were on fire, and black smoke covered the entire airfield. And then the sounds of ambulances, fire engines, and other security and safety vehicles could be heard. Slowly we made our way back into the base, thinking that this surely meant the end of our work here. All six hangars appeared to be on fire, debris was everywhere, and the airfield, including the runway, was full of huge craters. Surely there was no way we could continue to work at this place.

"There will be no interruption of work here," the Commandant said. We start work right now! Clean up, put the fires out, and everybody back to his workstation!"

I had to hand it to the Commandant. It was amazing how fast the situation got under control. By the day's end, the fires were out and a lot of the debris was cleared from the apron in front of the hangars and off the runway. It was a miracle that no one was killed, and that there were only a few minor injuries, broken bones, minor burns, smoke inhalation and such. A later inventory showed that those bombers dropped about 1200 bombs, mostly incendiaries, and several 200 and 500-pounders. It was obvious what the target was: the hangars and the runway. The center of the bomb swath missed the row of hangars by only 50 feet. The airfield was full of bomb craters and airplane parts. But everything was back to the normal routine by the next morning.

Things did change afterwards. No longer were air raid sirens an invitation to a siesta, rather the whole airbase had to be evacuated. Planes were to be taken off the apron and out of the hangers and scattered about the airfield, as far apart from each other as possible. Then everyone was to take any piece of rolling stock and drive it off the base into the surrounding countryside.

An antiaircraft battery of specially trained gunners was brought in, and all along the periphery of the field, machine gun trenches were dug out and manned by the German workers during air raids. To protect buildings on the airbase and the farmhouses along the country road bordering the western side of the airfield, all machine guns had governors on them to prevent them firing below a certain level.

Soon after D-Day, the Americans would send fighter plane sorties into the countryside. Just about every couple of weeks, two or three Mustangs would swoop over the field and spray the field with bullets. Quite often they would appear unannounced, without warning, and always they swooped in from the western side of the airfield, screened from view by the trees bordering the country road. Apparently the American fliers had the situation well scouted out. Come from the west, come in low, in between the houses and the trees. They would sweep across the field no more than 40 feet off the ground, wagging their wings, guns blazing. Before the gunners in the trenches had a chance to open fire, the planes would be gone. During the entire time I was on the base, the Germans did not hit a single plane.

While it was always the Americans flying these sorties, at least one time we had a totally unannounced and completely surprising visit by two British Mosquitoes, the light twin engine fighter bombers. It was on a beautiful, sunny summer day late in the afternoon. I just happened to be working on a Heinkel-111 bomber, high on a scaffold, when I heard the rat-tat-tat of machine guns. Usually no one particularly noticed the sound, because it was a common occurrence to hear the gunshots from the gunnery range where planes were being fitted with armaments. But this time the sound was distinctly different. When another burst of gunfire came, I looked up to see where it was coming from, and there between the hangars, low to the ground came two planes with guns blazing. Before I could even move, I saw the planes practically at eye level whiz by no more than 50 feet from me, and then I saw the unmistakable bull's eye insignia of the RAF. The planes completed their sweep over the field and disappeared into the sky. The whole thing took less than a few seconds. The Mosquitoes left behind more than a dozen planes in flames.

One truly tragic reminder of the real war was an incident similar to the first bombing raid on the airbase, except this time the straggling bombers dropped their load in the middle of Erding. Apparently they had not been able to hit their main targets up north because of poor visibility, so they unloaded on the way home. All of us, the Germans and foreign workers, rushed into town to help with rescue and whatever else we could do to help the people in town. I vividly remember a scene where a house received a direct hit, and the entire two-story home was nothing but a pile of smoldering rubble. A bloodied man, dazed and in shock, was digging frantically through the rubble, crying, "Meine Familie, meine Familie!"

We started digging into the rubble with nothing but bare hands. All of a sudden we heard a baby's cry. There in the pile of rubble we saw a body of a woman with an infant in her arms. A beam wedged over her body saved the baby but crushed the woman to death. The poor man had lost his entire family of several children and his parents. The only survivors of the family were the father and his infant child. I could not help but feel sorry for the man and for all the people of Erding. And again I saw the cruelty and the insanity of war. Are we ever to learn that wars solve nothing?

Another sobering aspect of the insanity of war was driven home for me with shocking reality. For a couple of weeks I was assigned to a salvage crew whose job it was to pick up and bring back to the airbase the remains of the shot down American bombers. Our first salvage involved a B-17 bomber which was shot down during a bombing run on Munich. As we came on the scene, we saw the burned out wreckage broken into several pieces, and next to the main body of the plane there were three bodies of the crew. They were young boys about my own age, and they were the first Americans I saw during this war. They had paid their price for our freedom and democracy. In a very personal way, at that moment, I felt that they had died for me, so that I could be free some day. It was a very moving experience for me.

The saddest part of this experience for me came when, after we had picked up the bodies and took them to the nearest cemetery for burial, the Catholic priest there refused to bury the Americans there because he did not know if they were of the Catholic faith. What bigotry! We spent the rest of the day trying to find a cemetery that would accept these boys for burial. I do not know how this problem was finally settled because I was sent back to the recovery site. But I still remember the resentment I felt toward that clergyman who would deny a resting place to a person merely on the basis of his creed.

Chapter

6

The War after D-Day

By the middle of 1944, the fortunes of war were turning sour for the Germans. They had lost Africa by the end of 1942, and the Russians won the battle of Stalingrad just about the same time. The Russians began pushing the German armies back west, the Americans were moving through Italy, and then on June 6, the Allies opened the third front by invading France.

German newspapers were still reporting on the victories of the German armies, but hardly anyone really believed it. We saw a lot of long faces among our German "friends", and a real concern about the future of the Third Reich. Germany was being bombed mercilessly by the Allied forces, and there was a new phenomenon appearing all over Europe, even in Erding: German refugees! German armies and the civilian population were retreating ever deeper into the western part of the country, scared to death of the advancing Russian forces.

Since Africa was lost early that year, the airbase lost its value as a tactical airfield. The base was decommissioned as a military operation, and the Messerschmidt airplane manufacturer bought the airfield to convert it into an assembly plant for the new German jet fighter the ME-262. Everybody on the base was excited about the news. The propaganda machine hailed the arrival of the new "miracle weapon" as the salvation of the Third Reich. Now, they thought they could beat the Allies at their own game.

Right away two main hangars were being converted to an assembly line, where the new fighters were to be assembled. All the other hangars were used to store the parts for the new fighters: fuselage parts, wings, engines, electronics, landing gears and all other things needed to make the plane. Huge truckloads of parts were coming in every day.

Then finally, six of the new fighters were scheduled to fly into the Erding airbase. For the Germans it was just like Christmas in August! The fighters flew in, landed, and were immediately surrounded by the German officials, trying desperately to hide the aircraft from the view of us foreigners. We had to laugh at the idea. After all, weren't we going to be the ones to work on the assembly line?

Shortly, however, the novelty of the "miracle weapon" wore off, and everybody was busy converting the hangars to an assembly line. The irony of the whole affair was that, by the end of the war in April 1945, not one fighter plane was completed, and of the six fighters that had flown in, five had been crash-landed by the test pilots learning to fly the new jets.

Even in our Stalag things were happening. First, some of the barracks where the foreign labor force was housed were being taken over by the German refugee families. And just about every week or two, several of the foreign workers would disappear, trying to get back to their home countries. One weekend late in the fall of 1944, about a dozen of the Czech workers disappeared from the camp all at once.

The Commandant was furious. He called all the foreign workers together and told us about the need to keep on working to help the German armies to fight the enemies, to save the Fatherland, and to carry out the orders of the Fuhrer. And then he announced the new policy: work will continue seven days a week, fifty two weeks of the year. No free days, no vacations. Anyone caught in an attempt to escape will be sent to the Dachau concentration camp.

"We are your friends, we don't want you to end up in Dachau. We want you to be safe. We want all of you to sign a promise that you will not try to escape," said the commandant.

Well, that friendly gesture went over like a lead balloon. Everyone refused to sign. Since no one would sign the promise, they increased the number of guards and military police to keep an eye on everybody, and to make it more difficult for anyone to run away.

By now, the living conditions had worsened to the point that we were no longer given ration tickets. Instead, we had to take some of our meals in the Stalag mess hall. The breakfast consisted of a cup of awful tasting black "ersatz" coffee and a slice of bread. Lunch was a bowl of a thin, potato soup and a slice of bread. For our suppers we were issued once a week one small loaf of bread per man, and a small cup of margarine. Usually we ate the bread in one sitting, and then just "bayed at the moon" during the rest of the week.

But we found out that German farmers badly needed fuel for their tractors. Thus, every time we drove off the airbase with a tractor and trailer, to pick up spare parts from one of the outlying warehouses, we would fill up the tractor's large fuel tank, and then we would trade some of the gasoline with the farmers for potatoes, milk, vegetables, meat, bread, or whatever. That kept us going. That very year I prepared a wonderful Christmas Eve dinner for my roommates, wienerschnitzel and German potato salad, all from provisions supplied by our friends, the German farmers.

Early in 1945, about March, one of my friends, Honza, received a letter from home that his father was dying, and wanted to see his son. My friend went to the Commandant, asking for a few days' leave, so that he could be with his father. But his request was denied. When he told me that the Commandant refused to let him go home, I could not believe it.

"You're going home, no matter what, and I'll go with you," I told him. "We're going, guards or no guards!"

Our plan was to avoid the train station in Erding, because there were too many military policemen there checking everyone's papers. Without a signed paper from the Commandant we would not have a chance to get on the train. Instead, we decided to walk to a small whistle stop in the countryside, where there were no guards. There we could hail the train and get on board.

We started out around noon, pretending just to walk to town on our lunchtime to buy some bread. We carried no backpack, just a small satchel, so as not to attract attention from the guards. Dressed for work in overalls, we managed to get to the whistle stop in the middle of large fields and wide open meadows. There was no one else there. Soon the train appeared, heading towards the East and the Czech border. The plan was to get off the train at the last stop before the state borders and cross the border on foot during the night. When the train came closer, we hailed it, and sure enough it stopped. There were no passengers getting off. So far so good! We got on the last car and stood on the rear platform.

The weather was balmy for this time of year. As we stood on the platform, we were taking in the beauty of the surrounding countryside. There were fields and meadows, and here and there a small woodland. Beside the rails ran the country dirt road that we had come on from Erding. But no sooner had we breathed a sigh of relief for getting on the train safely, when we saw a cloud of dust about a couple of miles down that road. Then we recognized the Commandant's staff car, followed by a small troop carrier with about a half dozen armed troops. Soon the entourage reached the train, and then the Mercedes staff car sped up to the locomotive, with the Commandant shouting at the engineer to stop the train. Slowly the train came to a halt on the tracks in the middle of nowhere.

The Commandant jumped out of his car and ordered the troopers to dismount. A couple of them, with automatic weapons at the ready, boarded the first car of the train. Two more guards, along with the Commandant, started to run toward the last car. We knew that we had no chance to get away in this wide open countryside where there was no place to hide, and where the guards could see for miles around. We just stood on the platform and waited for the inevitable.

The first one to climb the platform was the Commandant himself. Out of breath, and with a look of gleeful satisfaction, he grabbed my arm and said: "Im Name des Gesetses, Sie sind verhaftet!" (In the name of the law, you are under arrest.)

By then, the other two armed guards got on and arrested Honza. When we got back to the squad car, the other two guards got off the train and came to where we were. The Commandant realized that in his haste and excitement he had forgotten to draw his gun, and that he had actually taken me without having his Lugger in hand. Nervously, he jerked the gun out of his holster, took the cartridge out of his belt, and started shoving the cartridge into the magazine. His hands were shaking so much, that he spilled the rounds and dropped the cartridge on the ground. I started to bend down to pick up the bullets, when he shouted, "Don't touch that!"

The other two guards shoved the barrels of their guns into my ribs. I had to laugh. Here was the Commandant, all flustered and proud as a peacock for arresting a couple of deserters. I imagine, from the way he acted, that we must have been the first people that he had ever arrested. When things finally quieted down, the people who had come to watch the show got back on, Commandant waved the train on, and the train continued on its way to the Czech border without us.

We were ordered to take our shoes off, take the belt out of our pants, and climb into the back seat of the Commandant's Mercedes with an armed guard on either side of us. We were not allowed to talk. But all the way to the airbase, the commandant was exulting in his exploit.

"Just like in a Hollywood movie," he was telling his guards, grinning from ear to ear.

I was disappointed that we did not make good our escape, not so much for my sake, but because Honza was not able to be with his family at a time when they needed him the most.

Back at the base, we were signed in, and locked in solitary cells in the guardhouse. The guards took away our satchels and kept our belts, but we got our shoes back. The accommodations were rather austere. The cell was about 8 by 5 feet, with a bare wooden bunk, a blanket, and a wooden shelf for a pillow, and in one corner stood a bucket. High above the bunk was a small window with iron bars, a bare light bulb hanging in the middle of the ceiling completed the furnishings.

Well, now! Things didn't look so good right then. I had no idea what was going to happen next. We were told nothing, but I remembered what the Commandant had told us a couple of months before. "If we catch you, you go to Dachau." Not a very bright prospect! I said my prayer, and I felt reassured that everything would work out all right.

The next morning I woke up stiff and sore. I was not quite used to a wooden mattress and a wooden pillow. I did not know where Honza was, but assumed he was somewhere in the same guardhouse. I could not hear or see anyone through the small peephole in the door. I just sat on the bunk, and did a few bends and stretches, just to limber up my stiff carcass. After a while I heard some commotion down the hall: my breakfast, black coffee (tasted like roasted acorns) and a slice of dry bread. But the coffee was hot and the bread was not too bad.

Around the middle of the morning, the warden came to take me to the commandant for a hearing of some kind. There were a bunch of officers there, as well as our commandant, but Honza was not there. Apparently they would question us separately to see if our stories would agree. They took down all kinds of personal information. Then they wanted to know why we ran away. That was easy. Honza had asked for a leave to visit his dying father, and his request was denied, so I had told him that I would run away with him, to give him my moral support. That's all I said. I was taken back to my cell and was told that a judge from Munich would be coming within a few days, and he would decide what would happen to us.

About four days later, as I was sitting in my cell, I heard the air raid sirens go off. The guard came to get all the prisoners out, to take them off the air base. There were only three of us: Honza, a Dutch worker who was caught nearby while running away from one of the huge labor camps around Munich, and I.

As was customary, all air base personnel left the field during an air raid. Most everyone always headed out north of the airfield, because, as I mentioned before, all attacks came from the west. But this time we had no choice in the matter. The guard took us out of the guardhouse and started going down the road, running alongside the western fence line of the base. He stopped just about a half-mile from the guardhouse. A small creek was running between the road and the fence. We found ourselves right between the row of farmhouses west of the road and the airfield, with the runway and the hangars east of the road. We tried to convince the guard that here, right in the line of attack, was not a very safe place to be. But the guard assured us that this was the safest place, because the machine guns positioned around the perimeter of the field had governors on them, which prevented them from firing on the houses.

Besides us, the Russian POW contingent of about 25 men was brought up in a truck to the same location. We waded across the shallow creek, climbed up the fairly steep bank on the east side of the creek, and sat down under some large trees growing along the banks of the creek. I wound up sitting next to a young Russian POW, sharing the trunk of a large oak tree. About a half hour later, we heard some airplanes overhead, approaching the field from the west. They were not strafing fighter planes, but bombers flying fairly high. And then we heard that now familiar sound of falling bombs.

Before we realized what was happening, we saw the carpet of bombs explode among the hangars and along the landing strip on the airfield. They were not the large bombs, but incendiaries, and the deadlier anti-personnel bombs that burst above ground, spraying deadly shrapnel. As the first bombs fell, the Russian and I jumped up and threw ourselves down the creek bank behind the big oak, lying shoulder to shoulder. No sooner did we hit the ground, when down came the next salvo of bombs, bursting all around, showering us with dirt, branches and debris. It was all over in just a few seconds.

When all was quiet, I shook the dirt off my back, and stuck my head over the bank. I could see black smoke, a bunch of people screaming for a medic, and people running around--pandemonium! I looked over to my side where my Russian ditch-mate was lying, poked him in the shoulder and told him it was ok now, it was over, and to get up. When he did not move, I rolled him over. A small hole in the center of his forehead told me that he was dead. This was the closest contact that I had, before or since, with the deadly game we call war. I called the guard, and together we moved the young Russian from the ditch to the truck in which he had come from his compound. I said to myself more earnestly than ever, that there but for the grace of God could have been I.

It was only about three days later that Honza and I were released from the guardhouse without any explanation, and sent back to work. But things never got quite back to normal after this second direct hit on the airfield. There were rumors of American armies moving ever closer to Erding, and rumors of thousands of German refugees, soldiers, and civilians running away from the advancing Russian armies. At night, we could hear bombs exploding in the distance, the booming of cannon and rockets, and allied fighter planes flying overhead.

We could see now that most German co-workers knew that the awful defeat was inevitable. They all hoped that the Americans would get to Erding before the Russians did. Several German officers visited our barracks at night, asking us to speak kindly to the American forces about their treatment of us in the Stalag and on the base at work. How things had changed!

And then the miracle of miracles! One evening late in April 1945, as we were walking from the base to our barracks, there in the middle of the road just outside the airbase was a single, small, solitary American tank, driving past the airbase. We all cheered and waved, but the tank kept going. Then we saw the tank turn around about a mile down the road, and come back. But again the tank did not stop, just kept moving on towards the middle of town. We knew then, that for us the war would soon be over. The only thing we did not know was how it would play out.

We knew that the Germans were mining the entire airbase, preparing to blow up the base, so that it would not fall intact into the Allied hands. The next morning we went to work as usual, but at the roll call, we were told that the airbase had ceased to operate, and that all foreign laborers were free to return home. While Germany had provided transportation for us to come to work for them, they had no way to get all of us back home.

"You are on your own! Go home!" But that was all we needed!

Chapter

7

Going Home

After being told that we were free to go home, we wasted no time. We went back to the Stalag, picked up a few things, and headed for the train station. But there were no trains leaving for Munich, because the rails and the station in Munich were both put out of service during the recent bombings. The stationmaster told us that the rail station in Freising, some 5 miles east of Erding, still had available train service. We struck out for Freising, but just as we were approaching the station, we saw American fighter planes strafing the train, which was under full steam, ready to leave. The raid put the engine out of commission. The stationmaster said that it was the last available train, and that there would be no more service available for days.

From that point on, we were pretty much dependent on hitchhiking or walking. We headed north of town toward the major highway leading east, towards Regensburg and beyond to the Czech border. When we finally made it to the highway, we saw an incredible sight. The roadway was clogged up in both directions by traffic of all kinds, including military convoys, horse-drawn carriages, hand carts, bicycles, motorcycles, and hordes of people. There were foreign workers who had been released from labor camps like ours, there were German refugee families, and German military units of all types, all disorganized and in a hasty retreat.

I don't remember any more exactly how we got anywhere. All I can recall is that somehow we managed to hitch a ride on various trucks and wagons from time to time. In between, we walked. There were occasional over-flights by American fighter planes, and even a couple of strafing runs against some of the larger German military units. Each time everybody would run for the ditches, waiting for the strafing to stop. Then, the carnage would be cleared by German tanks, which pushed the disabled vehicles off the road, and tried to keep traffic going. Somehow, we managed to make slow progress.

By late afternoon we reached Regensburg. The last bridge across the Danube River had been destroyed just that morning by General Patton's army. When we came to the river, we saw the German engineers putting up a pontoon bridge. We were told that it would be at least midnight before the traffic would be able to move across the river. We were ordered, along with everybody else, to seek shelter at a large warehouse nearby. The warehouse was full of refugees, but we managed to find a small piece of open ground, sat down, and prepared ourselves for a long wait.

There is a historic and interesting footnote to this story. The unit of Patton's army which blew up the bridge at Regensburg was commanded by Colonel Polk, a relative of the former U.S. president, James K. Polk. My wife, Marian, is also related on her mother's side to President Polk. We had an opportunity in 1997 to meet the wife and daughter of Colonel Polk at one of the Polk family reunions in Columbia, Tennessee. Mrs. Polk was amazed when I told her that I was there at Regensburg on the very same day when her husband had ordered the bridge to be blown up. I told her that I had been released from the German labor camp and was trying to make my way home.

Around midnight, we spotted a small convoy of about six military trucks. We were puzzled by the insignia on the trucks. They all seemed to have Russian stars. Then we found out that the convoy of empty trucks was driven by Ukrainians belonging to General Vlasov, the renegade Russian general who had fought with the German armies against the Russians. These Russians were heading for Prague, and they agreed to give us a ride. There were about a half-dozen of us who had made it this far. Since I needed to go to Jihlava, I got off shortly after we crossed the

Czech border, and went to the nearest railroad station. I was told there would be no train until the next morning. Having had very little sleep, I decided just to hang around the station and try to catch a few winks.

The next morning I got on a train going to Jihlava. The trip took most of the day. There was a lot of waiting on side tracks, letting German military trains go by. I witnessed another couple of strafings by American planes along the way, before the train got out of the western part of Bohemia. Finally, in the late afternoon I got to Jihlava, and then I walked all across the town from the station to our home.

It was about six o'clock when at last I rang the doorbell at the parsonage. It was my mother who answered the door. I must have looked a sight, since it took her a few seconds before she finally recognized me. I got a big hug and a bunch of kisses before she let me go. It was then, when I finally found myself at home, that I realized how tired I was. I don't even remember if I saw my father and my sister Jirina at that time. I had been on that hellish trek home for almost three days, without much to eat and with very little rest. Mom offered me something to eat, but I was even too tired to eat. So she offered me a small glass of wine. I drank the wine, got into bed, and slept for about 24 hours straight.

When I finally woke up, cleaned up, and ate my first meal in several days, I felt human again. My Dad, Mom and my sister caught me up on the news of the past two years, and we just enjoyed being together again.

The first thing I wanted to find out was if there was any news about what happened to Vasek after he escaped from the Stalag. I went to see his parents. They told me the tragic story. Vasek had made it to Switzerland all right, but then he disappeared without a trace on his way from Switzerland to join up with Tito's partisans in Yugoslavia.

The war was winding down. Germany had signed a truce, but the SS troops refused to honor the agreement and continued to fight on. General Patton's forces were on the western border of Czechoslovakia, and the Russian armies were knocking on Berlin's door. In the southern part of Europe, the infamous General Malinovski's army of Mongolian cutthroats, joined by Slovak partisans, were pushing ever closer towards Prague.

One evening around the first of May, the Malinovski armada pulled up to the outskirts of the city of Jihlava and sent a message to the SS garrison to declare Jihlava an open city. The Germans were given until 5 o'clock the next morning to respond. The SS refused the offer. The next morning, the Russians began lobbing shells into the middle of town. My sister and I decided, along with a lot of other people, to go into town to see what was going on.

After several salvos of shells, the Russians began their move to take the town. It looked like people from the whole town were in the square. By about 8 o'clock, we could hear the Russian tanks rolling through the streets toward the town square. Then, somewhere, in a small city park, the retreating SS troops had disabled one of the Russian tanks. After that, the tank columns stopped their advance to the square, and started shelling the houses on each side of every street they passed. The infantry followed, fighting house to house, throwing hand grenades, breaking into the houses, throwing furniture out of windows, setting fires. This went on for several hours, until the Russians caught up with the small group of the SS troops who had shot up the Russian tank. Slowly things quieted down, and the rest of the Russian army moved into town. There were trucks, rocket launchers, troop carriers, guns, supply vehicles. The strange thing to see was that practically all of the rolling stock was American made, with the exception of the heavy tanks and the "Katusha organs" (rocket launchers). There we saw first hand the benefits of the generous American lend-lease agreement with the Russians.

By mid-afternoon the battering ram of the assault troops had moved on, heading towards cities beyond Jihlava on the way to Prague. After that came the occupation army. What a contrast! The occupation troops were all Mongols. It looked like something out of the Middle Ages: Genghis Khan and his troops! All on horseback on small, longhaired Siberian ponies, the men with pointed, fur-trimmed hats, and always at a dead gallop, riding up and down the streets!

There was hardly any motorized equipment. The whole army was moving on horse-drawn carriages, piled up high with the spoils of war. There was elegant furniture, Persian rugs, grand pianos, steamer trunks, clothing, toilet seats, stoves, tools, agricultural equipment! And everything at a dead gallop! Mongols swarming all over town like maggots over carrion.

One of the Russian officers with his staff moved into our parsonage, and established his field command post in my father's office. My mother had to cook for all of the men, about a half dozen of them. And they, too, had stolen everything in sight, including my father's pocket watch!

My former scout leader had contacted as many of his former scouts as he could find, including myself, and organized the troop to help the Russians guard strategic locations, such as rail bridges, factories, schools, hospitals and such, against marauding German army units. So I spent most of my nights watching for German marauders, and guarding former SS barracks against looters and saboteurs. It took couple of months before the Mongols left town. They left the town in quite a mess.

While all of this was happening, in the western part of the country General Patton's armies were moving into Bohemia, aiming their thrust toward the liberation of Prague. They freed Pilsen, the major population center and an industrial hub in the western region of Bohemia. Expecting an early arrival of

General Patton's army, people in Prague began to rise up against the dug-in SS troops, building barricades in the streets and attempting to oust the German forces. In the meantime, the Supreme Commander of the Allied Forces in Europe, General Eisenhower, issued an order to General Patton to stay out of the city of Prague because the Yalta agreement gave the Russians the sole right to liberate Prague. General Patton's forces, then already within a stone's throw of Prague, had to pull back to allow the Russians to claim Prague. In our country, that was considered one of the biggest strategic blunders of World War II. But, of course, everyone knew that it was not a military, but clearly a political decision.

Finally, on the morning of May 7, 1945, Germany capitulated and surrendered Berlin to the Allied forces. But not so in Prague! The SS troops fought the Russians and the Czech partisans as late as the next day, May 8. But ultimately, the former Czechoslovakia was a free Republic once again.

Chapter

8

A New Beginning

With the Russian army gone, we all started to look forward to a brighter future. I helped out at home, cleaning up after the Russians, visiting friends, and generally taking it easy. I spent some time with my relatives in Herspice, my father's hometown, mostly helping with farm chores. But I was anxious to start college to get my forestry education. The universities were being reopened, and the classes were to start in the fall.

Then something happened that I considered rather insignificant at the time, but in retrospect it became a rather prophetic and life changing event for me. Mother thought that it was about time for me to start looking for my future wife. She invited a daughter of her lifelong best friend to spend a weekend at our home. Her name was Hermina. She was a nice girl alright, but I just was not in the hunt. I took Hermina out on the town, took her out for walks, and tried to entertain her as best as I could, but my heart just was not in it. After the weekend, Hermina went home probably feeling as relieved as I was. But my mother was quite disappointed.

I felt sorry for my mother, because I knew she meant well. Then I remembered reading a World Christian Advocate a few days earlier, where I saw the family picture of Rev. and Mrs. Bartak. The accompanying article told about their upcoming return to Czechoslovakia, to resume their missionary work which was interrupted by the war. I took the magazine to my mother and showed her the picture. There was this beautiful young girl, their oldest daughter.

"See, Mom," I said, "That is the girl I'm going to marry. You don't need to worry anymore.

"Sure, and I'm a Pope," she replied. "Just how are you going to get together? She is in America and you are here!"

"Well, they're coming back to Czechoslovakia," I said. "Why not?" And nothing more was said about that incident for the rest of the summer.

In the fall of 1945, I enrolled in the "High School of Agricultural and Forest Engineering," the Czech equivalent of the College of Forestry. My brother, Vlasta, enrolled in the College of Electrical Engineering, both in Prague. We each applied for and received a monthly stipend of 2000 Czech crowns from the state, to defray the cost of tuition and living expenses.

The Central Methodist Church in Prague had some rooms available in their building suitable for lodging, which they made available to the children of Methodist ministers while attending college in Prague. So, Vlastik and I set up our housekeeping on the third floor of the church building, in a space once used as an office. But when we were asked where we lived, our standard answer was, "in the church, behind the organ."

Going to college in those days in Czechoslovakia was quite different. There were hardly any textbooks available, since all the old textbooks had been burned by the Nazis, so most of my study materials were just mimeographed pages of the professors' lectures. There was also a shortage of available space to hold classes, especially since my freshman class had over 1200 students. Most of the lectures were held in downtown movie houses and theaters.

To make up for lost time during the war, we were allowed to register for more than one semester at a time. I registered for all the subjects for two semesters at a time, and at the same time, my professors and I set a date for my final exam for each subject. Then I went home and studied at home. We were not required to attend classes, except for the labs and field exercises.

It was a hectic pace. My brother and I would study all day, every day, until about two o'clock at night. We only went out for lunch and dinner. Then at midnight we would cook another dinner meal on our hot plate. The menu was usually the same for each meal: chopped beef or mutton and potatoes. The canned meat came to us courtesy of the UNRA (United Nations Relief Association) packages.

But we always made time for MYF, or Youth Fellowship meetings, Sunday church services, and I even got involved in scouting. I became a District Scoutmaster with both boys' and girls scout troops.

Soon the life of a student fell into a routine. Get up, study, go to lab or to an exercise, go out to eat, come back and study. Bedtime usually was around one or two o'clock in the morning. And so it went, seemingly without any significant interruption, until the spring of 1946.

The family of Rev. Joseph Bartak then living in Houston, Texas, were making preparations for returning to Czechoslovakia after the war to continue their mission work. Their oldest daughter, Marian, the one I told my mother I would marry, was a freshman at Southwestern University where her father studied in the early 1900's.

Rev. Bartak returned to Prague in January 1946, and the plan was for the rest of the family, including Marian and her two younger siblings, Helen and Paul, to move back to Czechoslovakia in late summer. When Marian heard the family was to leave the U.S., she was not very happy about it.

"I love it here at Southwestern. I've made wonderful friends here, the school is nice, and everybody here is friendly. I just don't want to leave here," Marian told her mother.

"Our family has been so scattered throughout the war, your father was away from us for long periods of time," her mother said. "It would be nice to have the whole family together again. But I leave it up to you to decide."

"I know, I would like that, but this is a college where you can really meet some nice people," countered Marian. "Besides, I don't know anybody there anymore. Why can't I just stay here, and then I could go visit you there next the summer." She was determined to stay in America.

"Just think," her mother suggested, "you could study at one of the most prestigious universities in Europe, Charles University in Prague." Her mother tried to convince her that it would be a great experience to study abroad, something that many young Americans could only dream about.

When Marian told some of her friends about the possibility of going to Czechoslovakia, they also thought it would be an exciting experience.

"You may even find some handsome young man that you might like," suggested one of her friends.

"Well, it might be exciting and educational for me. But one thing I know, I don't want to marry any Czech fellow," Marian said emphatically. "I want to marry an American!"

Marian took a very long time thinking and praying about her future. Finally God laid it on her heart that, after all, it would be nice to be together as a whole family again, and worth a little sacrifice. The stage for God's plan for us was now set.

The World Council of Churches was planning the first, post-war, World Conference of Christian Youth to be held in Oslo, Norway in the summer of 1947. Announcements and invitations were sent ahead to all the Protestant churches throughout the world, asking them to send delegates to the conference. Delegates were required to speak at least one of the three official conference languages, English, German, or French. For that, my experience in the German labor camp became useful. Since I had acquired proficiency in the French and German languages during my stay in Germany, I thought that I might have a good chance to be chosen as a delegate to the conference. I listed French as my first choice.

To my pleasant surprise, my application was accepted and approved by the Methodist Superintendent, Dr. J. P. Bartak. Now I would have an opportunity to see yet another part of the world, and to meet a host of other young Christians from across the world. I could not help but reflect that, just one short year before, I had been sitting in a Nazi prison, contemplating an uncertain future. I felt strongly that my prayers from the prison cell were being answered in an unimaginable way.

In August 1946 came yet another unexpected gift from God. In one of our MYF meetings, SHE appeared. There in the flesh was the girl I had seen in the World Christian Advocate magazine, the one I had told my mother I would marry and she was even prettier in life than in the picture. The good Lord did not have to tell me twice: "Go get her!"

But then I realized that I could not speak English. How was I going to talk to her? But I felt the Lord would give me the words to say. Just go and talk to her. So I did. I remembered that way back, years ago, my mother was teaching us some English. Young girls are addressed as "Miss", and other ladies were addressed as "Mrs." The one syllable "Miss" did not sound as good or as important as the word "Mrs.", so I decided to use "Mrs."

"How do you do, Mrs.", I said, as I extended my hand. She laughed, and right away I knew that I blew it. But she just smiled, and said, "I am not Mrs., I'm just a Miss".

But from that moment on, every time I found myself in her presence, I stayed as close to her as I could without being too obvious. Now I was in the hunt.

After a while, I found that she was teaching a small English kindergarten class at our church for some English speaking children and Czech children whose parents wanted them to learn English. That gave me a chance to see her quite often, since I lived in the same church building. Later, however, she had to give up the kindergarten, as she herself began studies at Charles University. Well, one thing led to another, and soon we were going steady. We took walks in the park, down the street from where we both lived, I taught her how to ice skate again, and we went to the opera and to the zoo. Soon after we started going together, I asked her if she would teach me English. She said she would, if I would teach her French. We struck up a deal.

From that time on, I submerged myself in the English language. I read the English grammar text like one would read a novel, just to learn what it was all about. It seemed a lot easier than either Latin, Czech, German or French grammar. Then I started reading some English nursery books, and the Bible in English. I also attended English lectures at the American Information Service, and the English worship service, which Rev. Bartak held monthly at the church of St. Martin's-in the-Wall. At first, I could not understand much of what was being said, but I was learning, and getting used to the sounds and inflections of the language.

I knew that the most important thing in learning a new language is to start thinking in that language. So every time I would ride in the streetcar or walk somewhere, I would try to describe everything I saw around me in English. Quite often I would get strange looks from passers-by on the street, or from seatmates on the streetcar while I was mumbling English words under my breath. During all of this I was trying to teach Marian French. But I'm afraid that many times I used the hours for French lessons as an excuse just to be near her, rather than to teach. Every time we would end up speaking in English.

Anyway, the upshot of our arrangement was that by the next summer I spoke fairly fluent English, but Marian had not learned much French from me. Maybe she was a slow learner? But she was taking French courses in the French Institute nearby anyway.

By the time that the Conference of Christian Youth came closer, I spoke better English than either French or German. Here I was, with all the preliminary reports and papers to be given, the instructions and program notes for the Conference sent to me in French, and now I spoke better English.

When we departed for the Conference along with youth delegates from other Czech Protestant churches, God gave me the opportunity to spend even more time with Marian. She persuaded her father, the Superintendent, to let her go to the Conference as an observer. She was invited by the Norwegian Methodist Superintendent to stay with his family, while I was housed in the University of Oslo dormitory with other delegates.

The Conference was a great spiritual experience for both of us. I got to sing in the 300 voice Conference choir, met a lot of wonderful Christian young people, and shared in inspiring personal witnessing. There was one young Czech delegate who traveled with us, who was on his way to America to study for the ministry on a Crusade for Christ scholarship. He and some Americans we talked with were trying to convince me to go on to America, rather than to return to Czechoslovakia, because they were convinced that Czechoslovakia was going to go the way of the other Eastern European countries, which had become vassal states of Soviet Russia. To me that seemed unthinkable. The Czech nation had been allied with the Western civilization and culture ever since the beginning of recorded history. I saw no reason why Czechoslovakia would be willing to give up her newfound freedom. Czechoslovakia was a country founded on the principles of Western ideals of democratic government. It had a well established industrial sector, excellent agriculture, good education, and a high level of literacy. There was nothing the communist ideology could offer that would be more attractive to the Czech people than what they already had, I thought.

"No," I said, "that will never happen in Czechoslovakia. It will never fall for the lure of communism."

After our return from the World Conference of Christian Youth in the summer of 1947, our church hosted a group of American young people who came to Czechoslovakia on a mission trip. The group, called a "Youth Caravan", was under the sponsorship of Bishop Paul N. Garber. Superintendent Bartak arranged for the five members of the youth caravan to tour the country, visiting our Methodist churches, speaking and promoting the Methodist Youth Fellowship program among the young people. Marian and I were able to go along as hosts and interpreters, along with Rev. Bartak. It was a wonderful time for us, and a great spiritual experience for the members and youth of all the Methodist churches we visited. Large crowds turned out for the meetings.

Marian and I had become engaged in the spring of that year. As we discussed our plans for the future, it became clear to us that we would want to live in America. That meant that I would need a valid Czech passport and U.S. entry visa to emigrate. However, the law required that any Czech male wanting to emigrate must first serve out his compulsory military service. As a college student, I had a deferment from the military obligation until the completion of my studies. But at that time, I still had at least another year of college left to obtain the forest engineering degree. By that time I would be 25 years old, too old to "play soldier", I decided. So I made the fateful decision to interrupt my studies and enlist, and to serve my time in the army then, before I got any older.

Chapter
9

You're in the Army Now

I reported to my army post on October 1, 1947, in Brno, the capital city of Moravia. I don't remember what day of the week it was, but I do remember that I had to leave for Brno a day earlier in order to be there by 8:00 AM. I arrived on the afternoon of September 30 to report for my basic training. That first night as a recruit was a lonely experience. I had never felt more alone, since the time of my solitary confinement in Erding. But, for better or worse, there I was in the army. It did not take long before I realized that it would turn out far worse than I ever imagined.

Up early in the morning, calisthenics outside, no matter what the weather, breakfast, parade grounds, obstacle courses, weapons training, combat training, digging trenches, marching, running, jumping, and on and on, until you thought you couldn't take any more. You got dirty, your clothes were dirty, your weapons were dirty. The Sergeant yelled, "do this, do that, get cleaned up, fall in..." day after day, the same routine. The only difference was the Saturday inspection of the barracks. Everything had to be spotless and shipshape. Somehow one got used to the routine and endured. But it was never very exciting to me.

The only interesting time for me was the political education. Each day we spent one hour in the morning discussing current domestic and world problems, as well as the political trends of the day. I enjoyed the free give-and-take of the discussions, usually led by one of our sergeants, or some political officer. However, little did I realize that soon this experience would be my undoing.

By the time I got into the army, the political climate in Czechoslovakia had already begun to change, albeit almost imperceptibly. Even though the last parliamentary elections that summer were won by the more conservative democratic parties, the parties of the left, led by a resurgent communist party, had gained significant ground. The government was still in the control of the democratic bloc and we still had a free and democratic Republic. So I spoke "freely" during our political discussions about my dislike of totalitarian regimes like communism, fascism, and nazism.

"To me they are all alike," I said, "and we should reject any and all repressive forms of government which deny citizens the right of free speech, the right to worship according to one's conscience, and the right to seek one's fortune in an open, free market economy."

But the politically correct answer was always the same: "We must reject the capitalist philosophy and embrace the wonderful world of a share-and-share-alike society of our blood brothers, the Russians. We must hate our historical enemies, the Germans, and embrace with love our Russian brothers, who died by the thousands to make us free!"

"Well," I argued, "I am not prepared to hate anybody, and I am willing to offer my friendship to anyone, German, Russian, or American. That is what my God teaches me!"

There were not too many who converted to my point of view, but it made our discussions interesting.

While our political discussions in the army continued on a reasonably friendly level, on the outside the political situation seemed to be worsening. However, it did not seem to affect our army life. We went on with our basic training, and before I realized, it came to an end.

On our last day of training, we had a forced march exercise, combined with all sorts of combat encounters. Late that afternoon, while marching back to our barracks, I noticed that the captain of my group was slowing down until our platoon caught up with him. And then the bomb!

The captain fell in step with me, pulled me out of formation, and said that he had something he needed to talk to me about. He proceeded to share with me that the commanding officer of our post and his staff had decided that I was not politically desirable material, and that they would not allow me to go to the Officer Candidate School, to which college students were entitled. He told me that I was finishing my basic training at the top of my class, and that by all rights I had earned my entry into the O.C.S. But the top brass disagreed with my captain's position. I could not believe what I was hearing! I told the captain that I appreciated his telling me this, but that I really did not care one way or the other. However, he assured me that he would continue to insist that I be allowed to go to O.C.S. because I fully deserved it.

I felt betrayed, hurt, and I was quite angry. I knew right away what it was that got me in hot water, my stand on communism. But I could not believe that something like that could happen in our free, democratic country. As it turned out, my captain prevailed, and I graduated from my basic training and was going to the Officer Candidate School the very next day. It was a bittersweet victory for me, but I was grateful that at least one officer had the guts to stand up for my rights. Unfortunately, I did not get a chance to thank my captain. He was nowhere to be found. I have no idea what happened to him, but it would not surprise me if he, himself, was disciplined for speaking up for a so-called "politically unsavory character" like myself.

My troubles started as soon as I arrived in Milovice, a military base in central Bohemia, where the Officers' Candidate School was located. After we were received, processed, and were issued all of our gear, a feisty little Gypsy drill sergeant took my platoon to the barracks where we were to stay. Then he picked me, and told me to take the platoon and clean up the room, scrub the floors, wash the windows, and so on. I took the men and went to work. After a while, I told the men that we should all sing while we work.

"It'll make the work more fun," I said.

And the guys all started to sing and scrub, sweep, and wash. After a while our little Gypsy showed up again

"There will be no singing on the job!" he yelled.

"Why not? It makes it a lot easier when we sing. Let's sing, fellows," I told the group.

Well, apparently the little Gypsy sergeant did not like our singing. "You all shut up, and you," pointing at me, "you come with me!"

We went to see our lieutenant and, the sergeant told him that I had disobeyed his order. I smiled at the lieutenant, expecting some kind reply, but he saw no humor in the whole situation.

"Three days in the clink! Dismissed," he barked. He must have been suffering from indigestion, I thought.

So the little Gypsy escorted me to the jail and turned me over to the sarge in charge. In the cell, I began to make plans on how to go home for the weekend, because I had already promised Marian that I'd be home for the weekend. I said a little prayer, telling the Lord that I really don't understand the attitude of these army folks, that I don't really dislike them, but that they just do not understand me.

"And, Lord, can you show me how I can get home and keep my promise to Marian?"

I don't remember what it was I did, or told my jailer, but the long and short of it was that I got a three-day pass to go home and see my sweet Marian. Somehow the sergeant covered for me without any trouble.

There were many more incidents like this one to follow. I suspected that, somehow the people at the top must have known that I was not a great admirer of the communist doctrine. Why was it that every time we had an inspection, the sergeant or the lieutenant always took a beeline straight for me? Certainly it was not because I was a model soldier. Oh yes, I got more than my share of KP duty, and even time in the brig. But despite these misfortunes, and by the grace of God, I did manage to get along, and even make private first class.

On the outside the political situation was growing steadily worse. The communist party of Czechoslovakia, infiltrated by Russian-trained collaborators, took possession of the press, and took over the communication infrastructure to broadcast their communist propaganda. Early in February 1948, the Czech communists took control of Slovakia on the pretext, that the Slovaks were planning a revolt against the Czechs. Later in February, the communists threatened with a nationwide strike if their political demands were not met. President Benes countered by declaring the communist party illegal. The communists then seized the government ministries, and issued an ultimatum to President Benes to turn over the reins of the government to the puppet of the Moscow Politburo, Clement Gottwald. The ultimatum carried with it an almost insurmountable threat of takeover by force, to be implemented by Russian armies massed along the eastern borders of Czechoslovakia, if President Benes did not give in.

For the second time in the 20th century, my beloved country was betrayed by her "allies", who did not come to her aid. All that our "allies", the U.S., Britain, and France would do was to issue a condemnation of the communist coup, a mere slap on the wrist! And so, just as my friends in Oslo had predicted, on February 26, 1948, Czechoslovakia became a satellite of Soviet Russia. Less than a year before, I had argued vehemently that this could never happen. Oh, but how wrong I was!

Despite the political upheaval on the outside, I noticed very little change in my military life. Things seemed to go along as usual. One day shortly after the coup, I noticed a sizeable carbunkle forming on my right arm. I went to the infirmary to get some relief, but the doctor decided to send me to the military hospital in Prague, instead. That was just fine with me, because that would get me close to Marian. She visited me a couple of times during my one-week stay there.

On March 10, 1948, the communist newspaper, Rude Pravo, carried an article which claimed that on the day before the police had found the body of Jan Masaryk, the foreign minister and son of the first president of Czechoslovakia, lying in front of his Foreign Ministry office. That was only a couple of blocks away from the military hospital I was in. The paper said that Masaryk had committed suicide by jumping out of the window of his second story office.

Later that afternoon, I had a visit from a former college classmate, Zbynek Moravec. He, along with some other students, happened to come by the scene where the body of Masaryk was found. There was a large and angry crowd of Masaryk's supporters who were taunting the police, and accusing the communist secret police of killing the foreign minister and throwing him out of the window, to make it look like suicide. Zbynek told me that the autopsy performed by the doctor friend of his father had found two bullet wounds on Masaryk's body. The controversy continues even to this very day. No one in Czechoslovakia except the communists ever believed that Masaryk committed suicide. As I talked with Zbynek, he counseled me to leave Czechoslovakia right away, because soon the borders would be closed and no one would be allowed to leave. Even then, I still thought that he was being rather melodramatic about the whole situation. It was not too long before I found out for myself how right he was.

About a week after I returned to active duty, my platoon was carrying out some exercises, when a sergeant came to see our lieutenant. After a brief talk, the lieutenant came to me, saying that I was wanted at the headquarters. There, I was put under house arrest and taken to my barracks. At noon, I was taken to the mess hall, where the entire school was assembled for lunch. Another soldier, Vlado Bojsa and I, were taken under guard to the mess hall. We were escorted to the front of the assembly, facing a table full of military brass.

Then the unbelievable happened! The commander ordered everyone to stand at attention, and he proceeded to strip all military rank insignia and medals from the uniform of Vlado and myself.

"You have both been found politically unreliable and unworthy of wearing the uniform of an officer of the Czech army, and you are hereby dismissed from the Officers' Candidate School," the Commander said.

Vlado and I were drummed out of the corps like some traitors who had committed treason, and yet our only crime was that we did not like the communist party. We did not foment a revolution, we did not plot against the government, we merely spoke our minds. All of a sudden I realized how serious, and how deep was the trouble I had found myself in. I was seeing red! I could not believe this was happening. It was a good thing that I was not armed. At that moment, I honestly believe that I might have tried to shoot my way out of the mess hall.

Chapter
10
The Life of a Buck Private

The day after being booted out of Officers' Candidate School, Vlado and I were sent to a small military compound in Dacice, a small town in southern Moravia, near the Austrian border. By that time I had calmed down sufficiently to realize that any rash and impulsive action at this time was not the best solution to my problem. Rather, I resolved to simply serve my term as a buck private, not to raise any fuss, just do what I was told, nothing less, but nothing more. After all, I was not military career material. But the good Lord had other plans for me. He was going to make sure that I'd have some exciting times ahead.

The very first morning in Dacice dawned as a bright, sunny day. At roll call, a captain came and asked: "Is there anyone here who knows how to type?"

I had been told that you never volunteer for anything in the army, and I was not going to. But, somehow I heard myself saying, "I do. I can type."

"OK. Come with me," the captain said.

He took me upstairs, into the office of the commanding officer. The commander was an elderly major, a rather fatherly figure, and seemed quite friendly and harmless. The captain introduced me to the major, without mentioning anything about my status. He merely said that I was a recent transfer, again not referring to where I was transferred from or why.

The major and I shook hands. He said, that the three sergeants he had in his office were about to finish their tour of duty and were leaving within a week to go back to civilian life. He asked if I would be interested in working in the office. After he told me what the work entailed, I agreed to take the assignment. But I told the major that I could handle all the work by myself, and that he does not need three people to do the work. I don't remember exactly what his reply was to this brash statement, but he said, "You got the job!"

Thus a whole new chapter of my military service began. The job was really easy. In the mornings the officers would come into my office for a roll call and their daily assignments. They would all line up, I would go into the major's office to announce the officers, and the major would come in to take the roll call and give each officer his duty roster. After that I would go to the post office, bring in the mail, open the mail, sort it out, and take it into the major's office. Then I would file whatever needed filing.

Sometimes the major would come in to dictate a letter or two, we would talk about the weather, and whatever else the major wanted to talk about. It was a real plush job. After a week or two, I suggested to the major that it would really help if I could just move my bunk into the office from the barracks. I could help at night with the phone exchange across the hall when needed, and I could always be near the major for whatever he might need. To my surprise, the major did not resist very much. After just a couple of questions he approved the move.

I moved my bunk into the office, and I ate with the officers in the officers' mess downstairs. I was living on top of the world. The major and I became fairly close friends. He confided in me that he was about to retire, and that he was looking forward to his retirement. He admitted that he was not at all pleased with the recent political upheaval, and had decided to take an early retirement. The major was an avid fisherman and hunter. Several times in the afternoons, after most of the paperwork was done, he would come into my office and say, "Let's go fishing." So fishing we went.

The major had a good local merchant friend who owned a mill on a river and a grocery store in town. The man also had a young, nubile daughter that the major wanted me to entertain as a favor to his good friend. In the fall, during the hunting season,

70

the major wanted to go shoot some game. Always, he wanted to take the miller's daughter with us, so that I could sit in the blind with her, while he would sit in another blind waiting for a roe deer to appear. It was quite a life. I never imagined an army life like that.

It was on one such occasion when the major wanted me to entertain the miller's daughter that I told the major that I really was not at all interested in the girl, and that, in fact, I was engaged to be married the next year to my fiancee, Marian. One thing led to another, and the major found out that my fiancee was an American, a daughter of American Methodist missionaries. And I told the major that we were planning a formal wedding in the spring of 1949. He reminded me that as a soldier, I was not allowed to fraternize with foreigners, and especially the Americans. I explained that I had no intention of fraternizing with Marian, that I just wanted to marry her. Finally, the major gave up trying to explain how it is that I am not allowed to have any contacts with the Americans.

He added, "You know that, as a military person, you must be married in your military uniform. That's the law."

"But Major," I replied, "my fiancee is planning a formal, civilian, and church wedding. There's not much I can do about it. I just have to wear a tuxedo in my wedding."

The major did not seem to have much more to say. He just shrugged his shoulders and walked into his office, shaking his head, as if to say, why on earth did I ever get involved with this insubordinate!

Considering what had happened to me at the O.C.S. in Milovice, what was going on in my life in Dacice was a plain, unadulterated miracle. I felt very strongly the hand of the Lord in everything that was happening to me.

The local monastery in Dacice was preparing to celebrate a five-hundred-year anniversary. They commissioned a noted composer to write a celebratory mass for the occasion. The monastery was recruiting volunteers to help sing the mass. They came to the major, asking him to announce to the troops the need for singers. I don't remember whether or not there were any takers, but I know that I volunteered. The anniversary mass was beautiful beyond belief, and I enjoyed singing with such a wonderful choir and the organist composer. It was one of the most beautiful and inspiring experiences of my military life.

On another occasion, the local Little Theater group was looking for volunteers to take part in their plays. Again I volunteered, and took part in a musical called "The Village Princess", and also in the famous play, "RUR", written by the renowned Czech writer Karel Capek. As a matter of fact, I got so involved with the local Little Theater, that one of the leading members, the local postmaster, invited me to go on a judging junket with him, judging regional competitions among local theater groups participating in a nationwide competition of Little Theater groups. It was lots of fun.

It was during these trips to the local theater groups that my friend, the postmaster, asked me why it was that the political officer of my outfit had asked him to withhold all the mail addressed to me, and to keep it for him to pick up. And there was quite a bit of mail, too, because Marian and I were corresponding daily. I wrote letters in English, Marian would correct some of them and send them back all marked up, just as a teacher would mark papers, to correct misspellings and grammar. It was a wonderful way to study English. But when I found out what was going on with my mail, I asked the postmaster to give my mail to no one but me. And he did. From then on, the army did not get any more of my mail. Do you believe that was the Lord's doing? You'd have a hard time convincing me otherwise.

Then another interesting development or perhaps yet another miracle took place! One day, late in the afternoon, the captain who got me the job at the office came to me and struck up a conversation.

"I am the political officer of this post," he said, "and the army requires political officers to have a good command of at least two foreign languages. I speak German quite well, but I would like to learn English. I understand that you know English pretty well. Would you be willing to teach me?"

Obviously, I was taken aback by the request. In the first place, I had no idea until then that he was a political officer and wondered when the other shoe would drop. I had a pretty good idea how he had learned about my English; he was the one opening all my letters. But, to teach him? I had better think about that! Is it a trap he's setting for me, to compromise myself, or what? I thought about it for a moment, and then I said:

"OK, I'll teach you, but I won't do it for free. I'd like to be paid."

"That's no problem," the captain said. "Tell you what, you come to my house in the evening, we'll have supper, and then we can have our lesson, and you tell me how much you want for each lesson."

"All right then, it's a deal," and we actually shook hands on it.

A couple of days later we had our first lesson. I came to the captain's house, met his wife, and we sat down to have our supper. Everybody seemed rather tense. We ate our meal pretty much in silence. It was obvious that we were feeling each other out. The captain must have felt he's climbing out on a limb, and I, too, did not know what to expect. I could not bring myself to confide in the captain. He seemed friendly and sincere enough, but he was a political officer! I needed to play it safe. We had our first lesson, and I told the captain that he owed me ten crowns for the lesson. We shook hands again, and I went home to my bunk in the office.

Our next meeting started much the same way: a good meal, not much conversation, and on to the living room for our lesson. This time the captain closed the door behind us and then sat down at the table, next to me.

"Look," he said, "I need to clear the air. I know all about you. I know how and why you came here. You're not the first one who came here under a political cloud. People like you, the politically unreliable, are usually sent to special military labor camps, where they finish their military service and undergo political brainwashing. If they learn and change their attitude, they are discharged into society, but if they persist in their political heresy, they are sent to the uranium mines in Jachymov after completing their military obligation."

"That is where you, and your friend, Vlado, were heading from here when you were sent here for processing," he continued. "But I am trying to intercept such people and give them an opportunity to stay here, or if they are in real trouble, I take them across the border into Austria. But you are a special case. The army suspects you of being a spy, or an agent of some sort. Come to my office, I want to show you something."

When we got to his office, he went to a file cabinet, pulled out a drawer and said, "Come over here and look. This whole drawer is a dosier that the communist party has kept on you ever since you joined the army. Everything and anything you have said against the party is recorded here. All your mail has been copied and is filed here. There is a record of everything you did, whom you have seen, where you went. But the most intriguing evidence is in this letter here."

He pulled out a copy of a letter. The letter was from Marian's friend, Vivian, sent to her from Southwestern University in Georgetown, Texas. In the letter, Vivian was telling Marian about her college life, and among other things, about the sororities there. Of course, all the sororities use letters of the Greek alphabet for their names, and the communists must have gone ballistic, when they saw all those Greek letters. There it is, they thought, the evidence, the code! This letter is encoded as sure as shooting! All right, comrades, who speaks English? Who can tell us what's in this letter? Ah, no comrade could read English. Well, the next best thing was to copy the letter, put it in the file until we can find someone who can read it for us.

I could not help but laugh! Here was a drawer full of letters nobody could read, and now they wanted me to tell them what's in them. I told the captain I knew that they were intercepting my mail, and also told him that I put a stop to it. Now it was the captain's time to laugh. He knew that I knew, and he knew that it was I who had convinced the postmaster friend to give my mail only to me.

Now I knew where he stood and he knew my position, and I felt that I could trust him. Then I confided in my newly found friend about my plans to cross the border into Germany as soon as I completed my military obligation. He agreed that it was smart to wait until I was out of the service before going over the border. If I tried it while in the service and something should go wrong, I'd be shot on the spot as a deserter. Best to wait! But he offered to take me into Austria at any time my status would change, and I would need to get away. A coincidence, you say? That was no coincidence, that was God working yet another miracle on my behalf.

Not long after this amusing event, yet another incident worth telling took place. A military delegation from the Ministry of Defense announced an inspection of the Austrian border sector under our jurisdiction. A day before the delegation was to arrive the major had discovered that he had no up-to-date maps of the border sector showing the current location of all the fortifications, border crossings and guard posts.

He came to my office saying: "I've got a problem. We have no up-to-date maps of the border area showing the strategic locations, and I have no idea where to find a draftsman at this late date to do the necessary drawings."

"Not to worry, Major," I said, "I can do that for you. No problem."

"But we don't have enough time to get the job done before morning," the major lamented.

"Look, Major, there's another fellow in the outfit that can do the drafting work. His name is Vlado Bojsa. I am sure he would be glad to help. And if both of us get on it right away, and we work all through the night, you'll have your maps before the delegation gets here."

The major offered to pay us for the work, but I told him that I would rather have additional days of leave when I get married. Vlado also agreed to take extra leave in place of money.

When the major asked his officers to get us the necessary maps and information concerning the "top secret locations" of the guard posts and fortifications along the border, they were horrified.

"You are letting these two "political unreliables" handle top secret information?" one said.

"Yes, because we have no other option. Case closed!" retorted the major.

So Vlado and I set to work. We did finish the work by early morning, to the major's great relief. The inspection went off without a hitch, and the major was commended by the inspectors on the neat and accurate maps.

The work in my office went on. I took dictations from the major, filed papers, sorted the mail, wrote letters to Marian, and reread my letters that Marian returned to me with all the red ink, correcting my grammar and my spelling. Things were humming along.

The communist government was well entrenched in power by then, and it was not too long before we found out just how much power the comrades really had. Orders went out that citizens must give up all arms and ammunition, and that no one would be allowed to own arms. In Dacice, our post was given the responsibility to collect the arms. Guess who was given the job of receiving the arms and keeping a record of all confiscated items? I was the one! What irony! For weeks, people were coming to my office bringing all sorts of arms: old military rifles, shotguns, hand guns, even antique muzzle-loaders.

As I had already made up my plans for getting out of the country at the end of my military service, I thought it a good idea to have a hand gun to carry as I crossed the border, just in case. One day someone turned in a nice looking 0.36 caliber automatic that I thought would be an ideal gun for me. I managed to stash the handgun in my straw mattress for safe keeping.

It was about March, 1948, when I read in the paper that Czechoslovakia would again host the annual 50 kilometer walking marathon in August, 1948. The Praha to Podebrady marathon was an international race that had gained quite a reputation over the years, and usually attracted hundreds of athletes from home and abroad. I decided to enter, just like that, no training, no special conditioning. It was a good chance to go home, because by then my father was serving a church in Praha, and I would get a chance to see Marian as well. My captain and the major approved my request to enter the race in a military category, even though they were not quite convinced that I would even finish the race. I took this opportunity to take home my liberated handgun.

I got home on Friday night, before the Saturday race. I managed to see Marian, and she promised to see me again on Saturday in Podebrady at the finish line. What confidence that girl had!

Saturday morning, I got up around 5 o'clock, Mom fixed me a nice breakfast, and then I took a street car to the starting line on the eastern outskirts of town. I was wearing a lightweight field uniform, an empty cartridge belt, and my combat boots. The morning was sunny and cool, and the weather looked fine. When I arrived at the starting line, there were already hundreds of walkers milling around, getting checked in, and receiving instructions concerning the race. There were not too many participants in the military category.

Soon after the start of the race, I spotted a gray haired old man a few steps ahead of me, going at a pretty good clip. So I latched onto him and kept right alongside him for almost 25 or 30 kilometers.

As it turned out, this man was something of a celebrity. His name was Pesek, and he lived in Beroun, a small town about 25 kilometers west-southwest of Prague. This 65-year-old man had participated in this race every year for a number of years. He would walk from his home to Prague the day before the race, then walk in the race, and the following day he would walk back home. Quite a feat for a 65-year-old! And since he was a bit of a celebrity, I got my picture taken with him during the race. The picture made the national newspaper.

Well, I kept up the pace with the old man until I hit that infamous wall. For some reason, my second wind never showed up. Slowly, I began to lose my pacer until he disappeared out of my sight. But I fought over the wall eventually, and kept on plodding along. By the time I stumbled to the finish line, practically everyone was gone except the official timers. My time was about 5 hours and a few minutes, about 2 1/2 hours behind the winner, some world-class Hungarian marathoner. But I made it to the finish line, and I was proud of myself.

Marian was there as she promised and I was glad to see her. Once I stopped walking, I could hardly take another step. I sat down for a while on a bench, took off my ill-fitting combat boots, and looked at my feet. My socks were soaked with blood, and my feet were just one huge blister, bleeding profusely. After a while I made it to the showers, where I cleaned up, dressed in street clothes Marian had brought for me, and we took a train back to Prague. I did receive a medal for completing the race, and I vowed that I'd be back the next year and better my time. As it turned out, I did get to participate again in 1949, and I did finish a half-hour earlier, and without bloody feet. I still have both my medals. The race taught me a valuable lesson: "No matter what, just keep on putting one foot ahead of the other, don't look back, keep your eyes and mind on the finish, trust in the Lord, and you'll finish the race." So many times in my life the Lord has proved this lesson to me over and over.

Back in Dacice, my military service continued without much change. My friendship with the major deepened as we discussed current affairs, our hobbies and our future plans. He was to retire sometime early the next year to enjoy civilian life with his family and friends.

One night the major showed up in my office around midnight, rousted me out of my bed and said: "Get on the phone and call the officers. Tell them we'll have a readiness test with a forced march in full battle dress. Be ready in one hour!"

"Yes, sir! Right away, sir! By the way, would you like a cup of coffee while we wait?"

He looked at me as if he suspected some mischief, but then he nodded his approval, "Sounds good."

"I'll get down to the kitchen and get you a cup, sir, and then I'll alert the troops."

I made my way to the kitchen, got a cup of coffee for the major and a glass of milk for myself. Back in my office, the major and I sat on my bunk, sipping our coffee and milk. We started to talk about all sorts of things but the alert. Before long the major forgot all about the alert. I told him that was a good idea, and let's just not disturb the troops. We never did have that exercise.

My political officer, the captain, also became much friendlier, now that we understood each other. He was quite an active sportsman, excellent tennis player, champion table tennis player, hockey, volleyball, and soccer player. He got me to play on the army team in all those sports. I enjoyed the active participation, and especially the fact that I beat the captain once in a table tennis tournament.

Sometime shortly after my first walking marathon, Marian wrote that her university history class was planning a tour of some of the historic towns and castles, including a town in southern Moravia, not far from Dacice. Right away I suggested that I could meet her on the tour for a day, and we could at least spend one day together.

I did meet the group, and to my surprise, they were mostly foreign students studying at Charles University. We had a wonderful time. I enjoyed meeting many of the students as well as the professor who was guiding the tour. In fact, I had such a good time that I forgot about the time, and missed my bus ride back to Dacice. Never mind, so I was AWOL. The captain and the major would understand.

The next morning I caught the next bus to the base, but the captain was a bit put out about my being late. He said he really had no choice but to give me three days in the clink.

"That is just to keep up appearances. I can't afford to play favorites, you understand," he said. So into the clink I went.

In the afternoon of the same day, orders came to the base from the Ministry of Defense to participate in a National Day of Physical Fitness by organizing local mini-Olympics. We were to compete against civilian athletes in track and field events. The captain needed some-body to participate in a 5K run. When I found out about it, I volunteered.

"Look, sir. You need a runner, and I'll be glad to participate. Just let me out of jail for the race, and I'll come back after the race to finish my time," I offered.

After a while he said, "Well, I really don't have anyone else. We are supposed to have at least two or more military people in each event. Right now I am the only one in the 5K run. So you're it!"

So off I went to the race, and I am sure the captain was glad I volunteered. We finished one, two! And of course, I let the captain win. Later on, we were to play an exhibition game of volleyball against a Russian army team. Their team was the best of the best, since they were playing only to win, to show the superiority of the socialist regime in all endeavors. Well, we did not win that one; we did not even score a point against them.

Marian and I finally set our wedding day. It was to be April 16, 1949, Easter Saturday. We started making plans not only for the wedding, but also planning for the trip to America, once I finished military service. Marian went to the American Embassy about my entry visa to America. Her father had a good friend there. Since I did not have a passport to leave Czechoslovakia yet, my application would be kept on file to be approved once I would receive a valid passport.

Shortly before our wedding day, I reminded the major that he had promised me two extra days of leave for drafting all those maps of the Czechoslovak-Austrian borders. He remembered all right, but reminded me in turn about my obligation to be married in my military dress uniform, as dictated by the military code.

"I'll bring you the pictures of our wedding, so that you can at least see my beautiful bride," I promised, "and thanks for the extra time off." So instead of the customary two-day marriage leave, I had four days off.

On Saturday morning, on our wedding day, we went in Sunday dress to the historic city hall in the Old Town Square to take our vows before the magistrate, and sign the wedding book there, and to receive our marriage certificate. This was required by law, since the Methodist Church was not recognized as a national church. A church wedding alone would not be recognized as legal. As a matter of fact, the communist government later banned all church weddings in November 1950.

The actual wedding was a beautiful affair, held in our Central Methodist Church in Prague on Saturday afternoon. Marian wore a white wedding gown and veil, and I wore a black tuxedo. Rev. V. Vancura, one of the Superintendents of the Methodist Church, walked the bride to the altar. We had both of our fathers officiating, and the ritual was conducted both in English and Czech. My father and my sister sang a beautiful duet of "Always" in English, and Vlastik played the wedding march on the organ. Marian had her mother and some of her relatives on her father's side present, as well as many friends from our church congregation. Her sister and brother were still in America. My side of the family included only my father and mother, my older brother, Vlastik, his wife Jirina, and my younger sister, Jirina. The bridesmaids and groomsmen were our friends from the church, and the two young flower girls were the daughters of Marian's upstairs neighbor.

After the church ceremony we had the reception in the church fellowship hall. For our short honeymoon, we were loaned a villa on the outskirts of Prague for the weekend, owned by Rev. V. Vancura, who drove us there in his car.

After that, there were only five and a half months of military service left for me. I returned to Dacice, and as I had promised, I showed the major my wedding pictures.

"Isn't she beautiful?" I asked.

"Yes, she is. The very best to both of you," he replied. And to his credit, he never did mention anything about my tuxedo, just grinned a bit, as if he knew it all along.

Chapter
11
Five Months to Go

In May 1949, the major announced his retirement at the end of the month. My friend, the captain, came by to see me, offering to take me across the border into Austria upon completion of my military stint. But, as I had told him before, I was not at all anxious to jump out of the frying pan into the fire, and end up in the Russian occupied zone there. My plan was to cross the border into Western Germany, there was no question about that.

In the meantime, my father-in-law, Rev. J. P. Bartak was also taking an active part in planning my exit from Czechoslovakia. One of our church members, Mr. Wolf, formerly involved in the underground activities during the war, was now a postal worker, who also had been working on work brigades at logging camps in the border areas of southwestern Bohemia. There he had been able to acquaint himself with the exact location of the border, the strength of the border guards, and the scheduling of the guards. He had been able to take several people across the border into West Germany, including his own 14-year-old son. He probably received some compensation to supplement his meager wages. He approached my father-in-law, offering to help me across the border as well, and they made a deal. To this day I do not know the details they agreed upon. It seemed that everything was in place now, the plans firmed up, the date set.

Meanwhile, in Dacice my job was nearing an end, but not without some excitement. When the major announced his retirement, everybody was wondering who would take his place.

Finally, my friend the captain told me that the rumor had it that he would be replaced by some highly placed officer from the Ministry of Defense who was being demoted for political reasons as politically untrustworthy. In other words, he was in the same boat as I was, a kindred soul.

Soon the rumors were confirmed. The new commanding officer was Colonel Dedicik, a highly-decorated WWII veteran, who had fought with the English army and was married to an English socialite. A big fish, coming to a very small pond! This colonel, for good and obvious reasons, was not nearly as approachable as the good old major had been. He was courteous, but distant. I continued to serve him, performing the same duties as before.

About a month after Col. Dedicik came to Dacice, he and the captain went to inspect our sector of the Austrian border. After a couple of days, the captain came back, alone. Dedicik had disappeared. Later, the captain confided in me that the colonel had sent his English wife back to England, and now he himself was on his way to join her. He was telling the story simply to remind me how dangerous it is in such situations for people to leave the country. So many cases cropped up where the Secret Police started watching the remaining spouses, often arresting them when they tried to follow the spouse who had left.

I thanked the captain for the warning and told him that we were already aware of the situation. I told the captain that in our case I planned to leave first, most likely on my way home from Dacice upon my release from the army, heading straight across the border without even stopping at home to see my parents. And my wife would follow the very next day, before I would be missed. Under the communist regime, when changing locations, one had to report to the police any move from one town to another within 24 hours. Furthermore, I believed that because my wife was an American citizen, she might not be watched as closely as I would have been. It seemed that finally everything was in place for the great finale. But the Lord was going to test my resolve and patience one more time.

After Colonel Dedicik's disappearance, one of the senior officers at the post, another staff captain took over as the commanding officer. Since now I had only a little more than a couple of months to serve, I asked to be relieved of my post as a clerk in the office of the commanding officer and to be returned to regular duty as a buck private. Besides, our outfit was to participate in large, regional war games, on maneuvers in the Bezkydy Mountains in northern Moravia, and I thought it would be great to finish my military service with an all-expense-paid extensive "camping trip". The maneuvers lasted about a couple of weeks, and I really enjoyed myself: beautiful mountains, good food, and good company.

Upon our return from the maneuvers, there was another surprise awaiting us. Our outfit was to get brand new barracks. The post would be built by the army engineers, and the construction was to begin within a week or so. Most of us ended up working on the project as cheap labor, but I did not mind. It was out of doors, and it was good physical exercise, good for toning up for my upcoming long walk across the border.

But with only a couple of weeks of my service obligation left, I almost blew my future into oblivion. As usual, we were working on the site of the new post, excavating foundations with a pick and shovel, no less. As soon as our noon break approached, one of the captains from the Army engineers approached us. To my surprise, the captain was my former scoutmaster from Jihlava.

Another miracle, Lord? I think he was as surprised as I was, but since he knew me, he said: "I need a favor. We are about ready to pour some concrete over there," pointing to another section of the foundation, "and we need a few shovels to finish the ground preparation before we start pouring. Would you get me about six men with shovels and come over there to finish the job during the lunch break, so we can start pouring right after lunch? You do that for me, and you all can take the rest of the day off."

That sounded like a good deal to us. The six of us went with him to do whatever was needed. When we were finished, we went back to the barracks to enjoy the rest of the day. About an hour later, the sergeant showed up in our room.

"What are you guys doing here? You're supposed to be digging foundations on the site!" he hollered. We explained to him what the deal was, but he wasn't buying.

"I don't know anything about your deal. No one has told me anything about it. You'd better get your behinds out there, or I'll put you on report," he said, sounding a bit out of sorts.

Well, after that, the five other men decided they had better go back to work. They didn't like it, and grumbled under their breaths, but they went.

"How about you, private? That goes for you, too!" The sergeant said, getting more impatient.

"I am not going. The captain gave me the rest of the day off," I said, standing my ground.

"Suit yourself," he said, "I am putting you on report."

I didn't say anything, just turned around and went back to my bunk. In ten minutes the sergeant was back, this time with an armed guard.

"The captain wants to see you in his office. You'd better give me no trouble," the sarge growled. The three of us marched to the captain's office.

"What's all this about?" the captain asked me.

"Well, sir, I was given the afternoon off by the captain in charge of the building site," I answered, and proceeded to tell my story.

"I'm not interested in your story. I know nothing of such a deal, and you'd better get back on the job!" the captain said, not at all amused.

"But I got the afternoon off, Sir, and I am not going back, Sir," I stood my ground.

I was afraid the captain was having an apoplexy. His face turned ominously red, the veins on his neck bulging. He drew himself up from his chair, stood at attention and barked, his eyes bulging, "This is an order, private! You've got a choice. You go back to work, or you will be court-martialed! Do you read me?" Boy, was he some kind of mad.

As calmly as I could, not wanting him to have a heart attack, I said, "Sir, I will not go back to the work site. I have a..." I didn't finish the sentence.

The captain, now obviously upset, screamed, "You are under house arrest. You are not to leave your room, or the post. Get him out of here!" he shouted to the guard.

Walking between the sergeant and the guard, I went to my room and sat on the bunk. The sergeant reminded me again not to leave the room, and he posted a guard outside the room.

"Now you really cooked your goose, you dunce," I thought to myself. All the planning, and now a stupid show-off! Don't panic. Time for reflection! I really couldn't believe myself that I would jeopardize my future, my plans, my life, with such an uncalled for fit of pure inexcusable stupidity. I knew that the situation had gotten out of hand, and nothing short of a miracle now would get me out of this predicament. The next morning I was to be shipped to the state military prison in Brno, to await my arraignment and ultimate court-martial proceedings.

Dare I ask the Lord for yet another miracle, I wondered? As I prayed and thought, and prayed, slowly a plan was forming in my mind. I'll go to the captain, explain my situation, apologize for my disobedience of a direct order, and throw myself at his mercy. A pretty simple plan really, but there was a guard outside my door, and I had no guarantee that the captain would even see me. I agonized for hours, mulling over in my mind all kinds of other options, including such crazy ideas as an armed breakout.

Finally, about six o'clock that evening, I found myself at the door of the captain's living quarters, located a floor above our barracks. I cannot explain, nor do I recall how I got out of my room, past the guard, and stood there actually knocking on the captain's door. It all seems now like a dream, but there I was, waiting for someone to answer the door. Finally the door opened and I was looking at the captain's wife. At least, I assumed it was the captain's wife.

"Could I, please, see the captain, Ma'am? It's important that I see him," I said.

She let me in, took me to the living room, where the captain sat in an overstuffed chair, reading a newspaper. I have no recollection of how the conversation went. I felt like Moses before Pharaoh, and I believe to this day that it was the Lord who put words in my mouth. I heard myself telling the captain how I interrupted my college studies to join the army, got married while in the service, and how I already applied for admittance to college to complete my studies. And I don't know what else I might have said. Oh yes, I did apologize for my refusal to obey his order. I don't know how long I talked to the captain, or what he said.

All I remember is the captain saying to me at some point that he would tear up his report and forget that it ever happened. A miracle, pure and simple! An unruly, politically unreliable nobody, talking with a hard-line, card-carrying communist comrade captain, and asking his forgiveness! Just as the Lord promised, "Ask and you shall receive." I was literally handed a new lease on life! I cannot explain it, only acknowledge it. It was as if a boulder had been lifted from my shoulders. From that moment on, everything was back on schedule. Only one more week, and I'd be on my way home, and on my way to freedom in America. Needless to say, the last week passed quickly and without any other incidents. The mustering out day arrived, and miracle of miracles, I received an honorable discharge. Soon I was on the train heading for home.

Only 24 hours left then until my D-day, the departure day, I thought. The plan was to meet Mr. Wolf at some predetermined location and head for the border. If everything would go according to plan, I'd be in West Germany by the next night. My plans purposely avoided going home to see my parents, because I wanted them to be able to answer truthfully, should the State Secret Police ask them about my whereabouts. It was hard for me to do that, as I am sure it was for my parents and for my siblings. But I had talked about my plans more that once with my parents, and had explained my status as a "persona non grata" and "politically unreliable" person, married to an American, of all things. They well understood that my future in communist Czechoslovakia was less than bright. So we had all made peace with our arrangement, and put our trust in God.

It was late afternoon on Thursday when I arrived in Prague. I got off the train and walked home to the room Marian and I shared in her parent's apartment. Little did I expect to be greeted with the bad news. The border crossing was off for the next few days. Mr. Wolf had sent a coded telegram to his wife, who notified Marian's father that the section of the border where he had planned for me to cross was being fenced and mined, and that he would need a couple of days to find another place for a safe crossing. Now the crossing could not take place until Sunday at the earliest. That meant that I would have to remain incommunicado for the next two days, one whole day past the required 24 hours within which I should report my arrival to the local police station.

Obviously, our plans had to change. We decided I would stay in the apartment the entire time, until Sunday morning, the D-day. But on Friday, my parents called that they would expect Marian and me for dinner at noon on Saturday. There was no way to decline the invitation without raising suspicion. We decided to go see my parents, but would not tell them anything about my plans for leaving the country the very next morning.

On Friday we received a message that the crossing would definitely take place on Sunday. I was to take an early morning train to a small village in southern Bohemia, close to the 15-kilometer border zone, which no one was allowed to enter without a special permit. My guide would get on the same train at an outlying station in the suburbs of Prague.

Saturday was a difficult day for us. We went by streetcar to my parents' parsonage, and tried to pretend that everything was fine, but inside, our secret weighed heavily on our hearts. We talked mostly about my military experience, including my close brush with my court-martial threat.

"Well," my mother said, "maybe someday you'll learn how to control your mouth." If she only knew, I thought!

We managed to survive the dinner, but the hardest part of the visit came later, the good-bye! I knew that this could quite possibly be the last time I would ever see my parents and my brother and sister. I suspect that my mother somehow either knew what was going on with Marian and me, or at least had an inkling of what was about to happen. She held me in her arms for a long time before she let me go. We did not say much to each other, but our eyes were betraying both of us. My mother gave me a kiss and turned away, dabbing at her eyes, so that I would not see her cry. I said good-bye to my father and we embraced. Then I gave a big hug to my sister and my brother.

We left the parsonage in a subdued mood; we held hands and did not say much. Both of us knew about the impending separation, fraught with risk and danger. But we both felt that God was with us, and His love and grace would sustain us, no matter what would happen. When we arrived at home we busied ourselves with the final preparations for D-day.

Chapter

12

Day of Departure

The day was Sunday, October 1, 1949. The new plan was that I would leave in the morning by train, and cross the border on Sunday night, then find the nearest railroad station and catch a ride to Munich. There I would go to the American Embassy and leave an address where Marian could find me. Marian was to follow on Monday evening by train, and was to go the American Embassy to check for a message from me. A very simple and uncomplicated plan; the rub was only in the details. I promised Marian that I would try to meet her train which was to arrive in Munich about 6:30 on Tuesday morning.

At the last minute I decided it was best for me to go without any baggage. I would take only things I could carry on me or in my pockets, a watch, a compass, a flashlight, my ID document, and about ten dollars in American money. To be as inconspicuous as possible, I would wear my forest green outfit, pants and a zippered Eton type jacket that I had received in one of the shipments of clothing as part of the UNRA program. Originally I had planned to carry with me the 36 caliber handgun I had liberated in Dacice, but after considering the inherent danger of carrying an unlicensed gun, I decided against it.

We went to bed early that Saturday, because my train was leaving around 5 A.M. We got up about 3:30 A.M. Marian's mother fixed us breakfast, and Marian prepared a couple of sandwiches for me to take along. After the quick breakfast, we all prayed together, asking God's guidance and protection, and for peace of mind and heart for both of us. Then we embraced, kissed, and I went out of the door, down the stairway, and out into the street. It was dark, and the streets were empty. The city was still asleep.

I walked briskly up Jecna Street, turned west at the corner onto Stepanska Street, and headed for the main railroad station. I walked close to the buildings, trying to be as ordinary as possible. The only thing I heard was my heartbeat and my footsteps echoing through the empty streets. I didn't meet a single person until I reached the train station, just a block or two off Wenceslas Square. Inside the station I bought my ticket to the place of my destination, a name I no longer remember. I had about 10 minutes before the train would leave, so I bought a paper, got on the train, and waited for the train to depart. All the time, my eyes were scanning the surroundings for police, or any other suspicious or threatening persons. At last, the train began to move, slowly gathering speed, and finally pulling out of the station. The greatest adventure of my life had just begun.

There were only a few passengers on the train that I could see. It was Sunday, and very early in the morning. The train was a local, so it would stop at every station. About the second or third stop I saw Mr. Wolf getting into the car just ahead of mine. Only two or three other people got on the train. A few minutes later Mr. Wolf showed up in my car. When he saw me, he acknowledged my presence only by a hardly noticeable nod of his head, and proceeded past me, to sit down in the last seat in the car. We made no contact with each other the entire train ride.

Around 10 A.M. we reached our destination. By that time, the few passengers we had picked up along the way had gotten off the train. The station was a mere whistle stop, the last stop before entering the largely uninhabited border zone. As the train stopped, Mr. Wolf and I were the only two people getting off the train.

When the train pulled out we were alone. Mr. Wolf and I shook hands, and he asked, "Would you say a prayer for our safety before we set out?"

"Sure," I said. And then I prayed. As I prayed, I felt a sense of assurance and the promise of God's grace and His protection.

"Thank you," said Mr. Wolf, "let's go. We've got a long walk ahead of us." That was the last thing I remember that we said to each other until we approached the border later that afternoon. The first obstacle facing us was a small stream, the headwaters of the historic river, Vltava or Moldau, flowing alongside the railroad track. As we crossed the shallow stream, I felt like Joshua crossing the river Jordan into the promised land. I, too, felt that ahead of me was my promised land.

Shortly after fording the stream, we fell into the woods, beautiful stands of spruce and fir. From that point on, we never left the cover of the woods. Mr. Wolf knew the way quite well; he knew the locations of the border patrols, he knew the trails that the patrols used, and he knew their schedules. Whenever we would come near one of their trails, we would slow down or stop, waiting for the patrols to pass without us being seen.

It was a beautiful, bright, sunny October day. About noon, we stopped to rest and eat our sandwiches. By mid-afternoon, we came to the edge of the woods. Before us was a broad, shallow valley, with open meadows and old, abandoned fields. Across the valley, about a half-mile away, we could see the typical alley of fruit trees planted along both sides of a country road. By the road, there was a farmhouse, now empty, with several barns. About a hundred yards beyond the road was another dense stand of spruce and fir trees.

"That is the state border," Mr. Wolf said, pointing to the woods on the other side of the valley. "The border is just inside the timber stand, and it is marked by a low, stone wall, really just a pile of rocks. But that is the state border."

Then he told me that he had promised someone else to meet him later that afternoon, and that he would have to leave now in order to return in time to meet his contact.

"When crossing the meadow, try to stay away from that old farmstead. Sometimes the patrols use it as a watch post, or as a rest stop," he warned me. I told him not to worry about me, that I could take it from here, now that I knew exactly where the border was.

"But I ask one thing of you," I said. "Please tell Marian and her parents that you took me across the border. Don't tell them that you left me here. I'll make it for sure. Besides, even if I would not make it, Marian should continue on her way to America. Promise me that you will tell them that you saw me safely across."

He promised to deliver my message. We shook hands, and I thanked him for getting me there safely. Then he wished me a safe journey and God's blessing, and he was gone. I was all alone.

After Mr. Wolf left, I felt terribly alone. There was an almost eerie silence all around me. Nothing moved, no sounds, except an occasional chirp of a bird or the strum of a cricket. The sun was still high in the sky, the countryside was peaceful and lush, with green meadows surrounded by dark green forests on either side. I found a small thicket of young spruce and fir that provided a good cover. I crawled in, sat on the ground, leaned my back against a stout sapling, and looked at the scene laid out before me, trying to map out my route across that wide open space, step by step.

Straight ahead, about a half-mile distant was the border. There were not too many places where I could find cover, just an occasional shrub or a stunted tree. The rest was all open meadow. I decided that the best way to get there was in a straight line; wait for dark, and then head for the border. Easy enough! Once I had my route fixed in my mind, I settled back, and tried to rest and relax, and wait for the darkness to fall.

I had several hours to wait. My mind turned back in time, recalling my childhood, my growing up, the school years, the friends I had made along the way. All of a sudden I realized the immensity of what I was about to do. I might never again see my parents, my brother, my sister, or my many friends. I might never again see this beautiful land that was my home. Why? Just because I was not allowed to think for myself, to express my feelings about the oppressive form of government! My own people, my countrymen had declared me a traitor, an undesirable element in their society. I still felt some of the anger against my country that had turned against me. I knew that there was no future for me here. I had to get out and, hopefully, find a new country that would accept me, and give me an opportunity to live in freedom to pursue my ambitions in life.

From time to time doubts crept into my mind as I recalled Vasek, his escape to Switzerland, and then his disappearance as he tried to make his way across Germany to join Tito's partisans in Yugoslavia. And I recalled my own unsuccessful attempt to escape from the labor camp. Is that what lay ahead of me?

Those were very stressful hours for me. I prayed that my parents would understand and forgive me for the pain and heartache I would cause them by leaving my fatherland. But I felt that I was forced into it, that I had no other options, I had to get across the border. There was no future for Marian and me here, nor for that matter, for any of our future children.

Time passed agonizingly slowly. Everything around me seemed to be at peace. Inside, I was churning, my emotions running high. Finally, around six o'clock, I decided that I could wait no longer, that I'd just get up and run across the meadow to the border. I didn't see anyone or anything moving around all this time I was sitting there. The coast seemed clear. Time to go!

I crawled out of the thicket, took a few cautious steps towards the meadow. Suddenly a dog barked, and I heard the sound of human voices! Couldn't be anything but border guards! I dashed back into the thicket, hoping the dog had not yet picked up my scent. I lay down on the ground, my heart racing. I listened as the voices came closer. I could hear the give and take of a conversation, even though I could not understand what was being, said. Once or twice another dog barked. Finally the voices began to fade, and the conversation became more muted. They must have passed me by without noticing me. I breathed a deep, deep sigh of relief, and decided that I'd better go back to "Plan A" and wait until dark.

Around eight o'clock the skies finally began to darken. At about nine it seemed dark enough for me to see only about fifty feet, so I got up again and started to walk. And then another surprise! Out from behind a cloud came a bright, full autumn moon, a beautiful sight. In the bright moonlight I could see clearly all the way across the valley to the border. One could almost read in that bright light. My only recourse left was to get down on the ground into the thick, tall grass and crawl.

Slowly I made my way through the thick grass, searching for every bit of cover to hide in. From bush to bush, from tree to tree, I kept crawling. Then, as I was about to reach the bottom of the valley, the ground became increasingly softer, until I found myself in free water. I became soaking wet, but I pushed on, eyeing the long line of a deep, dark shadow on my left, cast by a low stone wall, which led up the hill toward the abandoned farmhouse. The wall was about fifty yards away, and I started to crawl toward it. Once I reached the wall, I felt relatively safe, as its shadow, cast by the bright moonlight was almost impenetrable. And I found that the wall was actually quite a bit higher than it had appeared from a distance.

Once in the shadow of the wall, I started to crawl on my hands and knees, making much faster progress. Soon I reached the end of the wall, as it made a sharp turn to the left, leading towards some farm buildings several yards away. By then, I could see the country road ahead of me, and the border beyond. I guessed that I was no more than a hundred yards away from the border and freedom.

In the relative safety of the wall's shadow, I decided to take a little rest to decide on the next course of action. After about fifteen minutes, it was time to move. By then the moon had disappeared behind a cloud and the darkness provided some measure of security.

I started to crawl again on my stomach through the grass, heading up toward the road. All at once, a dog barked! I heard the dog panting, circling slowly around me, his panting becoming louder and louder. If that is a guard dog, I thought, then the guards can't be too far behind. I froze to the ground. My heart was beating so hard in the stillness of the night, that I felt it could have been heard a mile away. What now! I was just a few yards from the road. My best chance, I thought, would be just to jump up and run for the border, no more than fifty or sixty yards away now. Maybe I could outrun the dog. The dog kept on panting, circling, closing in, and I felt my adrenaline rising.

Suddenly, to the right of me, almost within reach it seemed, a deer barked in fright, jumped over me, with the dog in pursuit, chasing after the deer. It took me several seconds to realize that this was not a guard dog, but just some hungry mutt looking for his supper. Where there's no guard dog, there are no guards. What are you waiting for, I told myself, the coast is clear, now is your chance, take it! I jumped to my feet, ran to the road, across it, and into the dark, dense forest and freedom. I reached the woods, and a few yards further I found the stone wall marking the actual border. I crawled over the mound of rocks, fell to my knees, and thanked God for seeing me through this far.

My original plan had been to get across the border, walk about a mile beyond the border, and find some sheltered spot in the woods and go to sleep. After all, I was already in about the fifteenth hour of my journey and feeling quite tired. It had sounded like a good plan, but circumstances called for a change in my plan. I was soaking wet, the mountain air was quite chilly, and I needed to keep on walking to keep warm.

The going was rough. I found myself in an old-growth spruce forest. It was dense, dark, and full of fallen dead trees. It was a jungle. I almost had to feel my way through the thick stand of trees. I would look at my compass to take a reading, head due south, and walk. It was a slow and painful walk, crawling, falling down, getting up and walking again. And every time I looked at my compass, I would be heading in the wrong direction. I would then correct my direction of travel and go on.

This went on for almost two hours. By now I began to doubt the accuracy of my compass. Surely I could walk five or ten minutes in a straight line! I could see no stars, could not find the North Star to verify my compass direction. My compass readings became more and more frequent, and my progress slower and slower. I had crossed the state line roughly at a 45-degree angle; that is, the border ran generally northwest to southeast, and my course was due south. If I were not able to maintain my southerly direction, I could easily wander back across the state line into Czechoslovakia. Despite my lack of faith in the accuracy of my compass, I decided that it was the only way to stay on course. So I kept on, checked the compass, walked, crawled, fell, climbed, and then checked the compass again.

Around eleven o'clock, as I was fighting my way through the woods, I heard the sound of rushing water. The closer I came, the louder the noise became, until I reached the bank of some stream. I could even smell the water! I felt with my hands for the water, but could not reach it. I couldn't see or feel anything but empty space below my feet, and hear the roar of water rushing down a slope. In the still of the night it sounded like I was standing at the Niagara Falls. I tried to walk up and down the bank of the stream, feeling for the water, but could not reach water anywhere. Because I wasn't sure how far from the border I was, I was afraid to use my flashlight, lest I attract the attention of some border guards.

After about a half hour of fruitless effort to find some way across this "chasm", I finally got on my knees, pulled my jacket over my head close to the bank, and shone the flashlight down on the stream. As frustrated as I was about the unsuccessful search for a crossing, I had to laugh when I saw the creek; it was deep all right, but barely three feet wide. I stepped over the creek, took another compass reading, and continued to make my way through the woods. The ground was sloping towards the south now, but I was still not quite sure where I was with respect to the state border. Still I kept going. At least I felt somewhat reassured, that as long as I was heading down the hill, I was going in the right direction.

It was almost two o'clock in the morning when I finally came to a clearing in the forest with some fields, pastures, and a homestead. That was the first sign of habitation since leaving the train station some 18 hours before. For the first time, I saw the clear night sky with beautiful stars. I found the Big Dipper and Little Dipper constellations and the Polaris. The compass had been right on target all the time. As I started to make my way toward the house, I heard a dog barking, and after a few seconds, a light came on in the house. Although I felt reasonably sure by then that I was well inside Bavaria, I decided to stay in the woods and walk around the clearing, rather than walk through the fields and pasture.

The condition of the forest had improved rather dramatically by then, the forest was less dense, and the ground was clearer of woody debris. Obviously, it was a well managed forest, so the walking was much easier now. I kept to my southerly course and just kept on walking.

Around four o'clock that morning, I finally reached a paved road. As I walked up to the road I saw a small light a short distance away. There was a small village, really just a half-dozen houses, and a road sign, giving the name of the village. I no longer recall the full name of the village, but it ended in a typical German way with "...dorf", meaning village. I knew I had made it. It was then twenty-four hours from the time I had left Marian the morning before.

Then I spotted a building with a sign that read "Grenze Patroll" or border patrol. I decided to turn myself in to the authorities as a refugee, and let them do with me whatever it is they do with the likes of me. As it turned out, I could not rouse anyone at the guardhouse, so after about five minutes of banging on the door, I decided to give up that idea, and headed down the paved road.

The road led generally in a southerly direction and downhill. It was an easy walk now compared to the scramble through the thick woods. I kept on until sunup. About seven o'clock in the morning I came to another, somewhat larger village, with a garrison of American troops. I thought that this might be an even better opportunity to report my presence to the Americans, but I could not raise anyone there either. I walked back to the road and sat down on the curb, taking in the warm sunshine, and just resting my feet.

After a while I saw a bus coming down the road, and as it came closer, I saw a sign on the front of the bus giving the destination as Passau. Finally I could confirm that my trek across the border was pretty close to a straight line south from where I had left the train. I was proud of my orienteering accomplishment. I knew that Passau was on the railroad running between Munich and Zelezna Ruda in Southern Bohemia. Passau was where I had planned to catch the train for Munich. If I could still catch a train the same day, I could easily meet Marian the next day in Munich, as her train would arrive about six-thirty on Tuesday morning. Even though I was quite tired after the long walk through the night, I felt good about the way our plans were falling into place.

The good Lord had been with me every step of the way. He even made me sit down on that curb, where, apparently, the regular bus stop was. I was a bit surprised when the bus pulled up to the curb to let off a couple of passengers.

I got on the bus and asked the driver, "Could you please take me to the railroad station in Passau? I don't have any German money, to pay the fare, but I could pay you in U.S. dollars."

At first the driver said that they were not allowed to take U.S. money, but after I explained my situation to him, he agreed to take me to Passau. And he took a couple of dollars, more as a souvenir, I think, than as bus fare. So the last 10 miles of my 25 mile trek across the border I finished in the luxury of a bus ride.

The driver dropped me off at the Banhoff in Passau, and wished me good luck. I thanked him again for the ride and headed for the station. The first thing I looked for was a washroom. I must have been a sight. I washed up and cleaned up as well as I could, and went to the currency exchange window. I had about eight dollars left after I had paid the bus driver.

"I would like some German marks, please," I said, as I stepped to the window.

"Your passport, please," said the official.

"I don't have a passport, only my Czech ID. I just crossed the border last night, and am on my way to meet my American wife in Munich."

"That's all right, sir. Here are your German marks."

I thanked the man and left with the money to look for a train schedule. I found that the only train to Munich would be leaving around 4 o'clock that afternoon, arriving in Munich about 8 or 9 that night. I bought a ticket and still had some money left. I went to a snack bar and bought some rolls and a piece of sausage, sat on a bench, and ate my first meal as a free man. A man without a country, but free. It felt good.

As I was sitting there, I could not help but think of the miracle that had transpired in the last twenty-four hours. I had only ten dollars with me. I really had no idea how much money I would need to buy a railroad ticket to Munich. The Lord fed thousands with only two fishes and five loaves. My ten dollars paid my bus fare, bought me some refreshments, and still I had enough left for my train fare. I just thanked the Lord, and told myself, "Don't worry about anything, just keep the faith."

I spent the rest of my time in Passau walking around the old medieval town with quaint shops and beautiful parks. When the time came to leave, I went to the station, got on the train, and headed for Munich. Once I reached Munich, it felt like being home, because I remembered the railroad station and the surrounding area from my visits there during my time in Erding. It was then about 36 hours since my adventure trek had started.

In Munich, I walked across the street from the station to a hotel, hoping to find a room. The desk clerk there informed me that the hotel was reserved for American military personnel, and that there was no room available. But after I told him my story, and the fact that I had not slept for 36 hours, he finally let me have a little cubbyhole of a room, way up in the attic. And he did not charge me anything for the room. I thanked him, went up to the room, took a shower and got into bed, glad that I had a place near the rail station, so that I would be able to meet Marian's train the next morning. The minute my head hit the pillow, I fell asleep.

When I woke up the next morning, it was almost 10 o'clock. I had missed the train! I knew Marian must have been worried when I didn't meet her train as I had promised. But I realized that we had made alternate plans for just such an event. We were to go to the American Embassy and leave information for each other, where we could be contacted.

I got the address of the American Embassy from the telephone directory at the hotel. After asking the clerk for directions, I took a streetcar to get there. At the embassy I went to the information desk and asked the clerk if by any chance Marian had stopped by.

"No," she said, "I'm sorry, but I don't remember anyone by that name."

Now I began to worry about Marian. She was a stranger in town and did not speak German. Was she able to find a place to stay, did she get someone to help with her luggage? It was early yet, so I decided to leave my name and address with the clerk and come back later.

Chapter

13

Trouble at the Border

At about the same time Mr. Wolf and I got off the train, back at home that Sunday morning, the Bartak family was getting ready to go to the worship service. I could see Marian and her parents in my mind's eye, praying for God's guidance and protection. And I knew that God was in control.

"I don't think I should go to the service this morning," Marian told her mother. "People will be asking about Barry and I don't want to be telling lies about his whereabouts. It would not be wise to talk about what's going on anyway, because we don't know who might be listening."

"I understand," her mother said, "You stay at home and rest. You have a rough day ahead of you."

After her parents left for the service, Marian was left alone in the apartment. In her mind she went over our plans for the next few days. Her part of the plan was more risky than mine. Most of what I had to do was done in secret. No one else knew about my current whereabouts, at least up to that moment, and the crossing was to take place under cover of darkness, hopefully without anyone around..

By contrast, everything Marian needed to do had to be done out in the open, navigating a dangerous network of communist rules and regulations without raising any suspicions. We both knew stories of other couples where one spouse was a Czech national and the other a foreigner. As soon as it became known that one spouse was missing, the remaining spouse would find himself or herself under much closer surveillance and scrutiny by the state police, and without any chance of ever being allowed to leave the country legally.

Our plan was for me to leave first, during the relatively safe period of 24 hours during which everyone moving from one place to another had to register his new location with the local police. Then, even if the state police would find out that I was missing, the state could not keep Marian, an American citizen, from leaving the country without creating an international incident.

Anyone leaving the country, citizen or foreigner, was required by the Customs Service to submit a complete list of all belongings to be taken out of the country three weeks prior to departure. Not wanting to raise any suspicions about our plans, Marian decided to take a chance and carry the list of belongings with her, and show it to the customs officers at the border. She knew about some other foreign students who had done the same thing without any problems. But just taking this chance must have weighed heavily on her mind. To ease her worry, she spent much time reading the Bible and praying for my safety, and asking God for her own peace of mind and heart. She kept herself busy organizing her belongings for the trip the next day.

As it turned out, her staying away from the worship service did not spare her or her parents from facing some anxious moments and probing questions. That very morning her cousin Martha came back from the worship service with Marian's mother to visit and to ask about me. Somehow Marian managed to answer her questions without arousing any suspicion. Fortunately, her cousin Martha did not stay very long. But there was more to come.

The next morning, on Monday, more unexpected visitors showed up at the door causing even more mental anguish and stress. First, Mr. Wolf surprised everyone by showing up at the door. He came in person to deliver his report on our trip to the border. Marian invited him to come in, and ushered him into the small dining room.

"I left Barry about a half-mile away from the border, but in clear sight of it," he told them. How shocking this must have been to everyone! But he hastened to explain:

"I had another previous engagement where I had to help someone. Barry made me promise him that I would tell you I saw him safely across the border. He assured me that he would make it across, and not to worry. But I didn't want to lie to you, and I just felt that I had to tell you the truth." I can imagine how such news must have affected Marian's mind.

While they were listening to Mr. Wolf's report, the front doorbell rang. Mrs. Bartak went to answer the door, and there were my father, and my sister, Jirina, coming to visit. Mrs. Bartak invited them to come in and took them by another door to the living room. Then she came to tell Marian to go speak to them. After that her mother escorted Mr. Wolf out of the apartment through another door. No one wanted my father and sister to find out at this time that I had already left the country, or to know about Mr. Wolf's involvement in my escape. That was to protect my family so that if they were questioned later by the authorities about my disappearance, they could say truthfully that they knew nothing about my departure. Also, if asked, they would not be able to identify who was the other visitor in the apartment that day. Mr. Wolf had helped a number of people across the border, and his identity had to be protected.

My father and sister came to see me, and Marian had to explain my absence without betraying the truth. It must have been a heart-wrenching experience for all. But I believe that my father and sister already suspected the truth.

Soon after they left, Marian went to town to get her exit visa, and then to the railroad station to buy the tickets for herself and for her mother, who planned to accompany her to the border. Then she returned home to finish packing and to get some rest before the long journey.

In the evening, Marian and her mother left for the train station. Marian had four large suitcases, packed mostly with our clothes and other belongings. Some of our wedding gifts, including a few pieces of Bohemian crystal and some embroidered scarves were packed among the clothes. But the most important contraband hidden among our belongings was a folder with our university documents, including credits earned. There were my documents from the College of Forestry, with the subjects I had completed, including my final grades for the six semesters of work I had finished.

Their trip to the Czech border was rather uneventful save for the tension and the dread of the unexpected. It was late at night when the train reached the border. Several customs and border officials came aboard the nearly empty train and soon reached the compartment occupied by Marian and her mother.

An officer looked at Marian's passport first. Her passport had been issued in her maiden name. The officer looked at the picture and then at her. Satisfied, he looked for the exit visa. When he reached the page with the valid visa stamp, Marian caught her breath, for on the very next page her married name had been added. But thankfully the officer was satisfied with seeing the exit visa, looked no farther, and handed her the passport. She breathed a sigh of relief.

Then he looked at her mother's passport. Mrs. Bartak told him that she only accompanied her daughter to the border and planned to go back to Prague on the next train. After hearing that, he asked her to step off the train and wait outside.

Several customs officers then came in. Marian showed them the list of contents of her suitcases. Only glancing at the list, one of the officials said, "Please open the suitcases."

Marian opened her suitcases and they began rummaging through them and scattering many of her things onto the benches in the compartment.

"You have some expensive items here," said one of the officers. "You should have obtained a permit to export these things."

"I did not buy any of them. They were gifts given to me," Marian replied.

"And there are some items of men's clothing in here," chimed in another officer, "who do they belong to?"

Thinking quickly, Marian told them that her brother had left the country some time earlier, but made sure that she did not say that they were his clothes.

Another official found Marian's folder holding all the university records and began leafing through it. Marian's heart almost stopped as she watched him paging through the papers. She prayed silently that he would not notice that some of the records belonged to someone else. Finally the officer closed the folder and handed it to Marian.

"It's obvious that you are carrying some things that belong to someone else," he said, pointing to her suitcases. "We ought to send you back to Prague."

The officials discussed among themselves what they should do with her. The lead officer decided to go back to the customs office and call Prague to see if she should be allowed to cross the border or be sent back.

After what seemed like an eternity, he came back and said, "You'll be allowed to continue your trip, but your mother has to go to the customs office with us and pay duty on the things you are taking with you." With that, the officials got off the train and signaled for the train to move out. Evidently they did not want to create an international incident.

The last thing that Marian saw was her mother being escorted to the customs office building between two guards, like some criminal. What a powerful statement about the political conditions of a once free people.

Marian could not hold back her tears anymore. She broke down and wept. All the pent-up emotions, tensions, the fear and stress, and the sudden realization of being alone in these strange circumstances, came pouring out in a flood of liberating tears. She was still sobbing as the train pulled into the German border station a few minutes later.

But what a difference there was between the arrogance of the communist officials, and the kindness and understanding of the officers of the free and democratic government of Western Germany. When these officials came to inspect her passport, they asked Marian why she was crying. Still sobbing, Marian tried to explain, but not being able to speak German, she just pointed to the scattered belongings spread out all over the compartment. And the tears kept coming. The whole incident with the Czech border officials, the worry about her mother and my escape was just too much. When she finally stopped sobbing, she began repacking her luggage and tried to get some sleep before arriving in Munich early the next morning.

The train arrived at the Munich Ostbahnhoff pretty much on time around 6:30 AM. Marian was disappointed when I was not there to meet her as I had promised, and she wondered if I had been able to get across safely at all. She decided that she would have to follow our alternate plan, to go to the American Embassy as soon as she could get settled in a hotel.

She found a porter to help with her luggage. He was able to check most of the suitcases at the station. But because she had no German marks to pay him for his services, she motioned to him to carry one suitcase and come with her to the hotel across the street. Little did she know that it was the same hotel where I was able to find a little cubbyhole of a room in the attic.

When Marian asked the desk clerk for a room, he told her the same thing he had told me, that the hotel was reserved only for the American military and their families. He gave her the name of another hotel several blocks away, and told her porter how to get there. At that hotel, the clerk told Marian that it would take some time to get a room ready for her, and suggested that she could have some breakfast in the dining room in the meantime.

Marian needed to exchange some American dollars for German marks to pay the porter and to buy her breakfast. The clerk said he could do that and took her to another room where he made the exchange. She was not quite sure how legitimate this back-room money exchange was, but at least she was able to pay the porter so he could return to the station. She also asked if the clerk knew when the American Embassy would open, and he replied that it was ten o'clock. That meant that she could have a leisurely breakfast and get some rest when the room was ready.

After a brief rest, Marian went to the lobby and asked for directions to the American Embassy. She found out which bus to take and what it would cost, and set out for the Embassy.

It was after ten when Marian arrived at the American Embassy. Already the reception room was swarming with crowds of people waiting to get permission and a visa to emigrate to the U.S.A. Marian asked the receptionist if anyone named Barry Malac had been there and left a message for her. The receptionist said that there were no messages, but since Marian was an American citizen, she could go to see the secretary in the next room. Once there, Marian explained the situation, and the secretary sent her to see the Vice Consul.

After hearing Marian's story, the Vice Consul said, "Bring your husband to see me as soon as you find him and we'll see what I can do to help you."

Marian thanked him and left the office, wondering how and when she would find me. She gave the secretary her name and the address of the hotel where she was staying, and also my name, in case I would come looking for her. Disappointed, Marian started to walk out through the crowded front reception room when she saw someone in a rumpled green jacket bending over the desk writing on a piece of paper and talking to the receptionist. Suddenly she recognized who it was. We fell into each other's arms, and both of us said, "Thank God you're here!" A miracle only God could grant.

Marian grabbed me by the arm, made a fast 180 degree turn and guided me straight back to the Vice Consul's office. We told him that I had previously applied for a visa at the U.S. Embassy in Prague, but since I did not have a valid passport, I could not receive a visa.

"That is the reason why I crossed the border night before last," I told the Vice Consul, "hoping that somehow I could be granted a visa here."

"Your case is not that rare," the Vice Consul replied. "We work with many refugees here. Let me call our embassy in Prague to verify your story and we'll take it from there. Since you are married to an American citizen, it should be easier for you to get permission."

After a few minutes of telephone conversation, he hung up the phone and said, "The American Embassy in Prague does have your paperwork. They will send it by the next courier. It should arrive sometime in the next three weeks. In the meantime you can arrange your passage."

Then he proceeded to fill out a "Military Travel Document" for me which would serve as a passport, a document that was then being issued to all refugees. Because I had been born in Vienna, Austria, he listed me as of "Austrian nationality" in it. I would also be able to go to the U.S. outside the yearly quota of immigrants, and under the "War Spouse Act," since I was married to an American. After I thanked the Vice Consul for his help, I was taken to an OSS office for debriefing.

When we finished with all the formalities, we returned to Marian's hotel. On the way we stopped at a small refreshment kiosk where I was introduced to my first taste of real America, my first Coca Cola! I still remember the taste. It tasted like freedom. At last I was free, and hopefully, soon on my way to my new country, America.

Chapter
14

Our Second Honeymoon

Here we were in Germany. All that we owned was in our four big suitcases. We did not have much, but we had each other, and we knew that God was with us. He had blessed us so much already, being with us on our separate and perilous journeys from behind the Iron Curtain into the free world. I had no money left at all, as I had spent the few dollars I'd taken with me for food and the train fare from Passau to Munich. But Marian had about $100, and a note from her father to get some money at a bank from his Swiss bank account, which should cover the cost of our travel to America. Now was the time to make our plans for surviving the three weeks in Germany, and securing our passage to America.

The first thing we had to do was to move as soon as possible out of the hotel where we were staying. In a day or two we were able to find a Pension where we could pay only $8 per night, instead of the $14 the hotel charged.

The second thing on our agenda was to book our passage on a ship to America. It proved not to be very promising. There was no air transportation available then, except for the military. Every travel office we tried said that there was no space available on ocean liners for at least four months or more, and we did not have enough money to wait that long. We became quite discouraged. Even at the last travel agency we visited, which was quite crowded with hopeful passengers, we got the same story. Disappointed, we turned around and began to make our way through the crowd to the door. Suddenly the phone rang, the clerk picked up, listened for a few moments, then broke out in a smile, and motioned for us to come back. We rushed back through the crowd to see him.

"We just had a cancellation, a second class cabin on the British ship Mauretania, sailing from LeHavre, on November 1," said the clerk. "The price is $400 for two."

We really wanted a cheaper tourist class passage, but since we could sail in about three weeks, we'd save on our stay here, so we could afford the $400 cabin. After thinking for a few moments, we said, "We'll take it. Thank you so much."

Having reserved the passage, we walked out of the office, realizing how much God had intervened in our lives again and again. We knew that God's spirit and His grace had again intervened on our behalf.

Since we had found a less expensive place to stay and had confirmation of our passage to America, we felt on top of the world. For us the world was at peace. We spent the rest of the day sightseeing.

We did more sightseeing the rest of that week. I took Marian to all the places in Munich that I had visited during the war when I got leave from the labor camp in Erding. We saw the zoo, the wonderful museum of natural sciences, art galleries, the beautiful cathedrals, the parks and more of the city. It was just a little more than four-and-a-half years since the end of the war, but the people of Munich had done a wonderful job of rebuilding much of their beautiful city. There were still plenty of reminders of the ugly side of the war though, bombed out buildings, and piles of rubble in many places. But to us it was like paradise. We were young, in love, and had nothing but a bright and sunny future ahead of us.

Our first Sunday in Munich, we decided to go to church. I knew the one and only Methodist Church that I had visited a couple of times while in Erding. I didn't know if the church building had survived the war, but I knew where it was. We found the church all right, and enjoyed the service. After the service, as we were going out, I introduced Marian and myself to the pastor. I told him that I was born in Vienna during the time when my father served a Methodist Church there. I also mentioned that Marian's father was the Superintendent of the Methodist Church in Prague.

To my surprise, when he heard the name Malac, he said he remembered a ministerial student by the same name in the seminary in Frankfurt am Mainz, and had served with him in the Austrian conference in Vienna. That man was my father. Well, one thing led to another, and soon we found that he had visited our parsonage in Vienna on several occasions when my mother was hosting a dinner for the conference clergy.

The pastor then invited us to have dinner with him and his family. At dinner we shared more of the details of our story with him, telling him of our concern about having enough money to pay for our stay in Germany, and the high cost of our passage to America. And yet again God was ready to solve our problems.

"Look," the pastor said, "our Church has a Conference Center near the Alps on a beautiful lake. It used to be a resort that the American army had used as its headquarters and later turned it over to our Church. We have a nice hostel there, and you can get a room and board there for about $2.00 a day. We have space available at this time. Let me call and make arrangements for you to stay there for as long as you need to. You can take the train back to Munich for any business you have to take care of."

"We'll be more than happy to accept the invitation," I said, thanking the minister for his kindness.

The very next day we moved by train to the Methodist Center. It was a lovely place in the foothills of the snowcapped Alps on a beautiful alpine lake. We spent about two weeks at this idyllic garden spot, recovering from the stress and strain of the last few weeks. This was a real honeymoon for Marian and me. The people there were very kind to us. Every day we thanked God for His goodness and for all the angels He had sent our way to encourage us, to strengthen us, and to show us over and over that anything is possible, as long as we put our trust in God.

We made a couple of brief visits to Munich by train during our stay, mostly to check on the progress of the paperwork for my visa. On our second trip we got the good news that the paperwork had arrived and my visa was granted. We were free to proceed with our plans to travel to America.

On October 31 we boarded a train in Munich, arriving in Paris in the afternoon. The rest of the day we did some sightseeing and spent the night in a hotel. Our ship was to sail from LeHavre about 10 P.M. the next day, and the boat train to LeHavre was to leave in mid-afternoon. Having more than half a day to spend before the boat train would leave, we decided to take a guided tour of Paris in the morning. We saw many famous sights and enjoyed a wonderful lunch at a street-side café.

After lunch we returned to our hotel, picked up our luggage and headed for the nearby subway station. We thought that would be the fastest way to get to the railroad station to catch the boat train to LeHavre, and at the same time to experience a ride on the famous Paris metro. No sooner did we get settled in our seats when to our horror we discovered that we were heading in the wrong direction, out of town instead of into town to the rail station. At the very next stop we scrambled out of the train with all our suitcases, and found out where to board the next train back. Needless to say, we did not enjoy the ride very much, since the boat train departure time was approaching fast.

We did make the train station at just about the time they were starting to close up the train, and we squeezed ourselves and our belongings on board. As the train was pulling out, we breathed a joint sigh of relief, and a prayer of thanks for getting on the train just in the nick of time. Can you imagine missing the train that we were working so hard to catch, our train to America? The good Lord must have been laughing himself silly:

"After all I have done to get you on that train, you almost missed it... What am I to do with you two?"

We arrived in LeHavre about 8 o'clock that evening and boarded the ship, the Mauretania. On board we had a sumptuous dinner at the captain's table while still at anchor. We enjoyed the sights of the harbor and the smell of the sea. I remember that very well, because that was to be my first and only meal that I had during the entire voyage.

The passage was rough. The North Atlantic Ocean gets quite stormy this time of year, as we found out. The next day I tried to get out on the deck on the advice of our steward, but the whole ship heaved so violently that I could not stand it any longer. I went below to our cabin and crawled into my bunk. My head was throbbing, my stomach churning. The ship kept bouncing like a cork in the heavy sea. I stayed in bed pretty much for the five days and nights of our trip.

On the last day, when the sea had finally calmed down, we started to prepare for disembarking in New York harbor. I made myself get up and get dressed, and even ventured out on the top deck. I desperately wanted to see the Statue of Liberty, the symbol of freedom for so many immigrants who had come before me. But the day was cloudy and the view of the New York skyline was quite dim, as fog and low clouds hovered over the harbor. Finally I caught a glimpse of "Lady Liberty", and I knew I was near the end of my journey. I breathed a prayer of thanks to God, who so graciously had led me through all the perils of this desperate journey. Here I was in America, my new home, and my new, brighter future. Despite the gray and murky sky, and despite the fact that I was weak from the ocean crossing, I looked forward to the future with hope, and with the assurance that God would not forsake me as long as I continue to keep my trust in Him.

Chapter

15

America, Here We Come

God did not wait too long before surprising us both with yet another miracle. As we disembarked from the ship, there on the pier was another of God's angels waiting for us. This time it was a young lady, a secretary from the office of the Board of Missions of the Methodist Church, waiting for us. She took care of getting us through the customs, secured a porter to help with our luggage, and took us in a taxi to the Prince George Hotel in downtown Manhattan, courtesy of the Board of Missions.

The Prince George was one of the ritziest hotels I had ever seen, elegant, ornate and gold-plated all over, it seemed. A liveried bellboy took us and our suitcases to our room, which seemed to be somewhere near the top of the building. I only remember the high speed elevator that shot up many stories in the blink of an eye, while my stomach was still languishing on the first floor. For a moment I felt seasick all over again.

After the bellhop deposited our luggage in the room, the angel from the Board of Missions gave him a tip and told us not to worry about anything, that everything was being taken care of by the Board. (A year or so later, when we were settled, we received and happily paid a bill for these expenses.) I don't think we did very much else that evening except go to bed exhausted, I slightly seasick, but grateful to God for His love and care, and thankful to be on terra firma.

The next day we went to the Missions office where we learned that a letter was waiting here for Marian from her Aunt Martha in Shiner, Texas. In the envelope, along with the letter was a hundred dollar bill. God knew that we had only about eight dollars left between us. We were to go to Houston, Texas, to stay with Marian's maiden Aunt Lucie Draper, and we had wondered how we would pay for the train tickets all the way to Houston. Here again, for the umpteenth time, was the miracle of God's prevenient grace.

That morning, my trip down the elevator made me a bit queasy again. But after some breakfast, my first meal since my last supper on board the Mauretania in LeHavre harbor, I felt reasonably well and refreshed and ready to take on the Big Apple. After some health exams by the doctor at the Board of Missions, which Marian's mother had arranged for us, we decided to do a little sightseeing. We saw Broadway, Fifth Avenue, Central Park, the Empire State Building, and all sorts of other interesting sights. And I was introduced to the great American institution, the hamburger.

All in all, we had a wonderful day in New York City. It really made a big impression on me. The smells, the sights, the sounds of New York are unique and unforgettable. When we got back to our hotel, I dreaded the elevator ride up to our room, but survived it with nothing more than a slight queasiness and a dizzy spell. Slowly, I was getting acclimated.

The following day we decided to look for my cousin on my mother's side of the family, Zdenek Navratil, who was supposed to be in New York studying theology and serving as an assistant at a Czech Presbyterian Church. Marian had the address and found the phone number of Rev. Sefl, who had come to New York from Chicago to serve that church. After a short bus ride, we arrived at the church, met the pastor and asked about my cousin, but he was no longer there.

"He became homesick," said the pastor, "and decided to return home to Czechoslovakia." I was disappointed that we could not meet with my cousin, but was even more surprised why anyone would want to go back to such a dreary existence.

The pastor invited us to look at the church and the premises. The church had a youth hostel where young people, like students, or people just starting out on their careers, could stay until they became financially independent. After hearing our story, the pastor offered us a room with two cots at the hostel, for just two dollars a day. That was a heavenly gift for us. We took him up on his offer and moved in the same day.

Altogether we spent about five days in New York, seeing the sites and enjoying the beautiful fall weather.We even splurged a bit on a show at the Radio City Music Hall, where the world famous Rockettes performed. I forgot what the movie was about, but I remember those beautiful Rockettes and their fantastic, precision high-stepping act.

Finally we decided that it was time for us to leave New York and head out to Texas. Even though our stay at the Presbyterian hostel was quite cheap, we needed to save money for the train ride. We made a reservation and bought the tickets for the two-day trip to Houston. The fare was only about $50 for both of us, so we still had some money left from Aunt Martha's gracious gift.

The day of our departure dawned overcast, cool and generally dreary, and not very promising for the long trip ahead. As I recall, we had to leave fairly early in the morning from Grand Central Station. We called for a taxi and made our way downstairs and out to the street. The streets were already getting crowded with the morning rush hour traffic, and we wondered if we would get to the train station on time. Finally an old beat up Yellow Cab pulled up to the entrance. A rough-looking driver got out and became very agitated when he saw all those suitcases.

"We're never going to get all these suitcases in. You'll need a bigger cab!" he grumbled.

I replied, "Get all you can into the trunk and put the rest in the back seat. I can sit on top of the suitcases if I have to. After some arguments and considerable huffing and puffing, he got everything loaded. Marian sat up front, and I squeezed into the back seat. It took at least fifteen precious minutes before the cabbie finally pulled out into the heavy traffic, blowing his horn and cussing at other drivers. I kept an anxious eye on my watch as I saw the time slipping away.

And then it happened! The cab came to a screeching halt, accompanied by a stream of profanity from the driver. The right front wheel had come off! But without missing a beat, our frustrated cabbie hailed another cab, and we transferred ourselves and the mountain of suitcases into the other taxi, and headed to Grand Central Station. We had two taxi cabs to pay for, but we were glad to be on our way.

Eventually we arrived at the station and found it as advertised, crowded with humanity, seemingly running amok. We found our train, got all our suitcases on board, and settled down in our seats with a huge sigh of blessed relief.

I came to America expecting to complete my forestry studies and to pursue my career as a professional forester. When he was back in Czechoslovakia on a visit, Bishop Garber had recommended to me the Duke University Forestry School in Durham, North Carolina. He told me that Duke University had one of the best schools of forestry, and in addition, that the Dean of the School of Forestry there was his close friend. The Bishop had been the Dean of the Divinity School at Duke before he became a bishop.

When we found out that our trip to Houston would take us through Durham, we decided to stop there and take this opportunity to visit the University and inquire about the possibility of some type of part time employment, and perhaps even of enrolling in the University. But evidently it was not part of God's plan for us at that time. There were no jobs available then at the University or in town, because most of the positions were already filled by students eligible for GI benefits, wives of students, or other people returning from the military ranks after the war.

We caught another train that afternoon to continue on to Houston. Some time the next morning we arrived in New Orleans, and had to wait at that busy rail crossroads to change trains. Finally we arrived in Houston, road-weary, bleary eyed, and ready to go to some place without wheels.

But we had yet another hurdle to clear. Once again we had to get a taxi, load up our earthly possessions, and head out for the terminus of our "great odyssey," which had begun a month and a half earlier in Prague, Czechoslovakia. It finally ended at Aunt Lucie's house on LaBranch Street in Houston, Texas.

We reached Aunt Lucie's house sometime in the afternoon. Marian's maiden Aunt Lucie, her mother's younger sister, was a sweet little lady who welcomed us to her comfortable house built by her father early in the twentieth century. This was to be our home for an undetermined time, a place of refuge and calm, and a symbol of true Southern hospitality. This was where Marian and I were to begin to establish ourselves as a new family unit. I felt that God had led us to this particular place for a yet not understood reason. The future lay ahead of us, not yet clearly visible, but promising, nevertheless, because we knew that God was with us. We placed our trust and our future into His care.

The first order of business was to find jobs to earn money for our support. Aunt Lucie took us to meet her oldest brother, Harvey Draper, who was a real estate agent for Kress Five and Ten Cent stores in Houston. Uncle Harvey and Aunt Mabel's house was nothing like Aunt Lucie's little house. It was a two story mansion, set in a well-to-do section, on a well-groomed lawn full of beautiful shrubbery, flowers, and moss-draped live oaks. For me this looked like the proverbial capitalist paradise.

When we arrived, we were met by Aunt Mabel. Originally from Tennessee, she was the personification of a gracious Southern lady. Her graying hair perfectly coiffed, with a big warm smile on her face, her Southern voice flowing like honey. She ushered us into the spacious and bright living room with French windows, offering a beautiful view of the garden full of autumn flowers. We met some other members of the Draper family, too many for me to remember. Of course, they all wanted to hear our story. To help with the story telling, Aunt Mabel brought us some iced tea and cookies.

After we shared our story, we confided in Uncle Harvey about our need for jobs. I think many of the folks there were taken aback when they heard that I was interested in a forestry career. Forestry? In Texas? The oil business was then the career of choice for Texans, or beef ranching, but forestry?! After the initial shock wore off, Uncle Harvey suggested that it might be a good idea for him to try to get me a spot on one of the local radio stations to tell my story, and let people know that I am looking for a job. After a while, and some more conversation, we started to leave. Aunt Mabel said she needed someone to wash the windows on their house. "Would you be interested?" she asked.

"Oh, yes Ma'am, I'd be happy to do that," I said. And that is how I got my first job.

The next day I came by bus to wash her windows. When I finished, Aunt Mabel gave me some refreshments, thanked me for a "job well done," and handed me a five dollar bill. The first American money I earned! I have never forgotten that feeling; and I could imagine God saying, "Atta boy," and giving a little chuckle.

I looked in the newspaper at a number of want ads, walked the streets looking for "Workers Wanted" signs in the windows, but without much success. A couple of days later Uncle Harvey got me an interview on a local radio show, and I actually received one phone call following that interview. An old lady who owned some rental properties in downtown

Houston was looking for a handyman to fix up her rental properties. I didn't know much about what was required of a handyman, I had no tools of my own, but I said I'd take the job.

The following day I found the lady in a slummy part of Houston, and told her that I was ready for work. I'm sure that she was not very impressed by a handyman without any tools, but she decided to give me a chance. She took me to one of her rental houses, a ramshackle, unpainted house with a sagging porch.

"I need to have the porch fixed up, and the stairs repaired. I have the lumber, and you can use my saw, hammer and nails," she said.

I thanked her for the job and the loan of the tools. Then she took me behind the house and showed me a pile of old, half-rotten lumber and said, "There is the lumber. The hammer, saw, and nails are in the bucket, here under the porch," and with that she left to run some errands.

I knew right away that this would not work too well. But I did my best to salvage as much lumber as I could to prop up the sagging porch, and to replace the broken and missing steps of the stairs. I believe the saw had never been sharpened. It was rusty, and it took forever to cut a piece of board with it. The nails were recycled, rusty old nails that I had to straighten with a hammer, which had a cracked wooden handle and a hammerhead that was continually falling off. When the lady came back that afternoon, I showed her what I did, and let her know that I would not be coming back. I did not want to hurt her feelings by insisting that she needed to buy new lumber and new nails to do a decent job of repairs. I did not charge her anything for my services, but thanked her for her kind offer.

The next day I saw an ad in the paper by a tree service company offering starting positions. I called in, and to my surprise, got an invitation for an interview. The man explained to me the nature of my job. I would need to go to a National Forest to dig up young saplings of live oaks, and then to go to the many new subdivisions to try to sell the trees to the new homeowners for $10 a tree. My commission was to be one dollar per tree. The selling aspect of the job did not appeal to me one bit, and besides, I was not quite sure that digging up seedlings on the National Forest was legal.

On Sunday we went with Aunt Lucie to her church, St. Luke Methodist Church, where Marian had been a member at one time. It was a huge church with several thousand members. We joined the choir where Aunt Lucie was singing, and enjoyed the worship service. After the worship service, we went to the fellowship hall for some refreshments, and there to our surprise, we met Roger Deschner, the youth director. We had first met Roger when he was a member of the North Carolina Youth Caravan mission team that came to Czechoslovakia in 1947. It was a pleasant surprise to see him again and we reminisced together about the wonderful experience we all had in our old country.

Rev. Joseph Dobes, another old acquaintance of ours, and his wife also lived in Houston. He had been one of the very first missionaries to Czechoslovakia, and he was also a distant cousin of my father. Until his retirement, Rev. Dobes had served as a Superintendent of the Methodist Church in Czechoslovakia. After he retired, he settled in Houston, and attended the First Methodist Church downtown, one of the largest churches in Texas. We contacted him by phone, and shared with him our story and my need for a job. He invited us over for dinner and a visit. He told us he knew a member of his church who was the president of Kirby Lumber Company, and he promised to mention my need for a job to him. I was offered a job with the lumber company, and Rev. Dobes and I were invited to attend the annual Christmas dinner held at the Corporate Headquarters in the Kirby Building in downtown Houston. God had opened yet another door for us, where there seemed to be so little hope.

Chapter
16
Humble Beginnings

I accepted the job in the forestry department of the Kirby Lumber Company, which managed about a half million acres of forest lands in Texas and Louisiana, owned jointly with the Santa Fe Railroad.The forestry department of the Kirby Lumber Company was headquartered in Silsbee, Texas, some 95 miles due east of Houston, and near the larger city of Beaumont, Texas. I was to start right away, and report to Silsbee, where I was to live in the company "hotel" located on the large mill site.

Meanwhile, Marian got a job as a Christmas sales clerk at Foley's Department Store in downtown Houston. So that she would not have to leave her job right away, we decided that she would stay in Houston with Aunt Lucie for the time being, and that I would go to Silsbee and look for an apartment, or house for us to rent. Then she would come to Silsbee to join me and we could really start our new life in America together. It all sounded so wonderful and promising.

Two weeks before Christmas I took a bus to Silsbee. The town was not much, just a typical, southern sawmill town. There were a couple of churches, a grocery store, filling station, hardware store, as usual for a small community. I asked for directions to the Kirby hotel and made my way there. When I spotted the "hotel" my heart sank. The hotel was a ramshackle barn-like, two story building, unpainted, and looked like it was about to collapse. I thought to myself, "What in the world did I get myself into?"

Slowly I walked up the creaky stairs leading to the entrance, knocked on the door. When I heard no answer, I opened the door and stepped inside. I found myself in a large room with a high ceiling, a couple of rows of long tables with wooden benches and two large potbelly stoves. Surrounding the stoves were clotheslines hung with pants, shirts, underwear, and muddy boots. It smelled like the Dallas Cowboys' locker room.

A plump and pleasant looking, middle-aged lady showed up, and inquired how she could help me.

"I was to report here, to the hotel. I got a job with the Company, and was told that I would be staying here," I told her. "My name is Barry Malac."

"Oh, yes, Mr. Denmon is expecting you. Let me show you to your room," and she started toward a large stairway leading up to the second story. I followed, taking in all the "exciting" surroundings, and wondering what "my room" would look like.

"This is your room, right here," the lady said, opening a door.

I stepped inside and looked around. It did not take but about ten seconds to inventory the entire room. It was a large room with the same high ceiling, a bare bulb hanging on an electric cord, a rusty metal bedstead beside a large, curtain-less French window, which must not have been washed since the hotel was built, and a single chair. That was it, such quaintly spartan furnishings.

"I hope you'll be comfortable," she said. "Breakfast is served at six, I fix you a bag lunch, and dinner is at six in the evening. Showers are downstairs. If you need anything, just ask." Then she handed me a large towel, wash cloth, and a bar of soap, closed the door and disappeared.

That evening I was introduced to the "boarding house etiquette, Texas style", and to my boarding house mates. They were tough, rough-looking woodsmen and workers in the large sawmill. There were about twenty of them, altogether. And all of them were real-life characters, but they all seemed friendly enough. They must have wondered what a skinny little runt like me (I weighed all of 135 pounds) was doing in a sawmill town. After supper we all sat around the stove and swapped stories, told jokes, and talked about everyday news. Then the men would gather their clothes off the lines and go to their respective rooms.

I went to bed that night wondering what tomorrow would bring. When I said my prayers that night, I confided to God that this, of all places, was not really what I had imagined to find in America. Just the same, I was thankful for the opportunity to prove myself, no matter the circumstances. I felt assured that God would provide whatever I should need.

The morning came with a blast! I sat up bolt upright in my bed, wondering what was going on. I had failed to see something the day before, partly because I was in a state of mild shock, and partly because I could not see through the dirty window by my bed. There, not more than five feet away from my bed, outside the window, was the mill whistle, announcing the arrival of a new day at 5 AM sharp. What an alarm clock! Only in America, I thought to myself.

After I got myself back together, I went downstairs to shower, then dressed, and went down again for breakfast. I had never seen a breakfast like that in my whole life: eggs, scrambled or fried, hot biscuits, honey, ham, grits, fried potatoes, sausage, sawmill gravy, pancakes, strap molasses, jelly, toasted bread, stewed apples, and I don't know what else. It was a breakfast feast. The hotel might not look like much, but the food was fabulous. That morning things did not look nearly as bad as they had looked the night before, and I knew that from this point on, things could only get better.

After breakfast, we all picked up our lunch bags and went our way. I took my bag and looked at what was in it: standard fare, a ham and egg sandwich, apple, an enormous chocolate chip cookie, and a napkin!

Mr. Denman showed up at just about that time, looking for me. He was a handsome looking man, about 50 years old, dressed for the out-of-doors, with a pleasant and reassuring smile.

We shook hands, and then he said, "It's nice to meet you. You'll be working with me and my crew as a timber marker. I understand that you've had some forestry experience, so that should be no problem for you. You'll be paid the starting wage of 75 cents an hour. We usually stay out all day and get back about 5 each evening. But before you meet the rest of the crew, I want to show you around the saw mill, and have you meet some of the people."

"Ok," I said, "I'm ready, and thank you."

We took a quick tour of the saw mill, and then stopped by the chief forester's office to meet him and some of the foresters. It was interesting that all the foresters there were the first graduates of a fairly new forestry school in Texas, the Stephen F. Austin Forestry School. I remember the names of only two of the men I met that day, Jim McMahon, the chief forester, and J. W. Valentine, a forester who was just hired that summer. I especially remember J.W., as he was called, because we became close friends, and he became my mentor and my guardian angel. He taught me how to drive, and loaned me his Ford pickup truck to take my driver's license test.

After finishing the tour of the mill, we walked out to the parking lot to meet the rest of the timber marking crew. They were a rough bunch of about four or five men, ranging in age from about my age to middle age. But they were friendly, and offered to help with anything I needed. We took off to the woods to select and mark trees to be cut. Finally I was in some familiar surroundings and doing the thing I loved the most, practicing forestry. I knew then that I was in the right place at the right time. The future looked bright and beckoning. God had put me where I needed to be, right at the bottom of the ladder. "Now show me what you can do." It felt so good, so right, and I could not wait to tell Marian that we were on the way.

I was introduced to one of the perils of American forestry after a couple of weeks on the job. On that day we were marking the timber in a natural stand of loblolly pine. The stand had quite a thick understory of brush hardwoods, vines and brambles. As I walked through the stand, looking up into the crowns of the tall trees to find the suitable tree to mark for cutting, my foot got caught in a vine and I fell down. In trying to soften my fall, I extended my left arm and fell to my knees. My arm landed about a foot away from the large coiled up pile of a snake. And then I heard it! The unmistakable rattle! Even though I had never seen a live rattlesnake before in my life, I knew right away what I saw and heard. Slowly I got up and backed away from the snake. I called out to my coworkers to come see the snake. One of the men dispatched the snake with a machete, and then they proceeded to skin the snake. Apparently the snake must have just shed his skin, because the distinctive diamond markings were showing in brilliant hues. The snake measured six feet four inches in length, and had about twelve rattles. Later in my career as a forester I met up with and dispatched many rattlesnakes, but not one of them matched the size of this Texas rattler. Inside the belly of the snake the men found three little rabbits. That was the most likely reason why the rattler did not strike at me, his belly was full and he was lethargic. The men were going to use the skin to make rattlesnake belts for themselves.

For my first Christmas in America, we were invited to visit Marian's aunt and uncle Chovanetz in Shiner, Texas. I was quite excited, and anxious to meet my new "family", since they were the ones who had signed the required affidavit for my visa, vouching for me, that I would not become a public nuisance. I took the bus to Houston a couple of days before the holidays, and after work on Christmas Eve, Marian's friend and former high school classmate, Madlyn, and her boy friend, took us with them in their car to Shiner. Aunt Martha and Uncle Charlie welcomed us, and me especially, as their own. They were both teachers at the two-room Bunjes School out in the country, had no children of their own, and so they lavished their love and hospitality on us. I felt very much at home.

We had a wonderful holiday in Shiner. Aunt Martha invited many of her friends to come and meet us, and arranged for me to talk to their Sunday School assembly on Sunday morning at the Shiner Methodist Church. It was a wonderful occasion, and we both felt encouraged and heartened by the tremendous outpouring of love and friendship from the community. Aunt Martha had even arranged for a belated wedding shower for us.

After the holidays Marian moved with me to Silsbee. At first we rented a small two room apartment close to the center of town. But we stayed there only for the two weeks I had pre-paid, because we discovered that the place was full of huge Texas roaches that made crunching sounds at night. Spraying them was not much help, because to them the spray was like dessert. They seemed to thrive on it.

We joined the local Methodist Church and joined the choir. As usual, we soon made many friends in our new church family, and they helped us to find another place to live. A widow lady owned a large old farmhouse on the edge of town, where she lived and provided two small apartments, each with a kitchen. We shared the bathroom with another young couple who had a small baby. Our apartment was plain, but adequate. We even had a small garden plot where we could grow some vegetables.

Soon Marian found a job as a secretary with an insurance company about 30 miles away in Beaumont, Texas. Fortunately, she also found a ride with a man from our church who was taking two other young women to work in Beaumont. Then with both of us working, we were making about $90 to $100 a month. Everything was coming up roses! After a month or two, we felt that we had saved enough money to buy a secondhand car.

We were referred to a reasonably good used car dealer in Beaumont, where we found a 1946 Oldsmobile four-door sedan. The salesman assured us that it was in good condition, and it did look pretty good to us. He told us that the car used to belong to a "little old lady who used it only on Sundays to drive to church."

Little did I know then what I know now about car salesmen and little old ladies driving their cars only on Sundays to church. We paid about $400 for the car and were happy to drive it home to Silsbee. Later on, I took Marian back to Beaumont to take the driving test to get a driver's license as well.

After some three or four months of my work on the tree-marking crew, Mr. Hunter, the company surveyor offered me a job on his crew. It paid 90 cents an hour; so that was a 20% raise for me. Incidentally, that was the biggest percentage pay raise I ever had throughout my entire working career. I jumped at the offer and started my new job the next week. It was a wonderful job, out of doors in the fresh air, involving some out of town, and even overnight travel, but I saw much more of the forest lands that the company owned and managed. My job was as the machete man, clearing the survey lines. It was hard work, often in swampy land, wading in water, waist deep and full of water moccasins and snapping alligator turtles.

By the next summer we decided that it was time for us to move on and get back into school to finish our college education. Marian lacked the senior year of college to graduate, and I needed to get my degree in forestry. I applied to the graduate School of Forestry at Duke University, and Marian planned first to get an office job so that we would have some income to live on. Since I had no official records from the forestry school in Prague, except my final exam records with the grades and signatures of the professors, which Marian had secretly carried out of Czechoslovakia, I prepared my own transcript in English, listing all the forestry courses I had taken and completed. I had the transcript notarized and submitted it to the Dean of the Forestry School. With a recommendation from Bishop Paul N. Garber, and based on my transcript, I was notified that I had a sufficient number of credits for a Bachelor Degree, and enough credits to satisfy about half of the needed coursework for the Master's degree. But since I had no official transcript I would be accepted for one semester on a trial basis as a "special student," and would be accepted as a full student after that, if my performance was satisfactory.

Marian's mother, then living in Houston, decided to come visit us in Silsbee and help us with the move to Durham, N.C. Both of us resigned our jobs and by mid-August 1950, packed up our Oldsmobile, and together with my mother-in-law, struck out for the mountains of North Carolina. It was really a wonderful trip, my first extended automobile trip in America. We experienced a lot of heat, rain, and mountainous roads through the Smoky Mountain National Park.

Chapter

17

Back to School

The first phase of our life in America behind us, we looked forward to starting our second phase, this time in academia. We were able to find a small, one room apartment with a kitchenette in an old house near Duke University campus, found a full time job for Marian at the University, and I obtained a working fellowship at the Forestry School.

Since I never had any formal training in the English language, I was afraid that I might have some difficulty with my graduate studies. I asked about taking some remedial course in English. I was told that Duke did not offer any such course, but that I could take freshman English instead. Very soon I found that I had no problem with my English, and was able to fully engage in classroom discussions and to communicate with my professors. My fellowship commitment allowed me to register for only 20 credit hours per semester, and to spend 20 hours per week working for the School. As it turned out, I spent my entire 20 hours a week drafting new maps for the Duke Experimental Forest, and the job pretty well paid for my tuition and books.

My class of some 90-plus students consisted mostly of men who had served in the military during WWII and were eligible to take advantage of the GI bill for their college education. It was a wonderful group of young men, many of them married like myself.

Most of these young men became the leaders of the forestry profession in America. Many of them became pioneers in forestry research in the universities, in the federal Forest Service, and in the burgeoning private forest industry. I have always maintained that my claim to fame was that I had some very famous people as my classmates at Duke School of Forestry. We made lots of lasting friends from all over America, friends that we cherish even to this day.

After several months, we found a larger apartment in a house down the block, owned by the same landlady. There we had a living room, bedroom, kitchen and bath. Then in 1951 my mother-in-law decided that she would like to come live in Durham for a while, to be near her daughter. Marian's sister, Helen, who was a junior at Southwestern University in Georgetown, Texas, also decided to transfer to Duke, so we had to find a still larger apartment. We found one even closer to the East campus, upstairs in a nice old Victorian house owned by a lovely old lady, Mrs. Moss. We rented the entire second floor, with two apartments.

In the summer, Marian's sister Helen, came from Texas, and Marian's brother, Paul, transferred from Texas State Teachers College in Huntsville, Texas, to N.C. State in Raleigh, for his sophomore year, to study animal husbandry. He would come see us in Durham on weekends. That fall, Marian also began her studies to complete her senior year of college at Duke.

By 1951, Marian's father, as an American citizen, was no longer allowed by the Czech communist government to preach and perform his duties as leader of the Methodist mission, and returned to the U.S. in 1952 for a sabbatical. He also came to live with us in Durham, when he was not traveling to speak in various churches. Finally we had Marian's whole family together, after so many years of separation.

Soon we both adjusted to the new experience of college life as a married couple. During the week we would attend classes, do part time work, and would share in the household responsibilities. On the weekends we were involved in the life of our church. We sang in the choir and attended Sunday School at Trinity Methodist Church in Durham, and in general took our place in that church family.

In December of 1952 I took the oath of citizenship in the District Court of Greensboro, North Carolina and became a U.S. citizen. As I received my certificate of naturalization, I thought back over the events of the last couple of years, leading up to the fateful moment: the betrayal by my own government; the fact that I was declared a traitor and an enemy of my country; the denial of my future as a citizen by my own country of Czechoslovakia that I loved; and then my determination to leave the country where I was not wanted. All of this was merely for disagreeing with the authoritarian and oppressive communist government. In the blink of an eye, as my military insignia was stripped from my uniform, I had become a man without rights, a man without a country. In my mind's eye I saw myself leaving Marian, leaving my family, my friends, then the risky border crossing, and my uncertain future in America. But all of this was finally behind me, and as I looked at that certificate in my hands, I knew that the future ahead of me was bright again and full of promise. With my lips and my heart I whispered a prayer of thanksgiving to God, who had never forsaken me, and who had brought me safely to this wonderful and exciting moment of my life.

At the close of the first semester, Dean Korstian of the forestry school informed me that my work was satisfactory, and that I would be registered as a regular student for the next semester. I inquired about the possibility of getting my bachelor degree, since I had enough credit hours to satisfy the requirement for it. But I was told that while I did have enough credits, I would need to satisfy the residency requirement by staying on campus for one additional year. So I decided not to seek the B.S. degree, and to use the extra year of residency to sign up for all the other courses required for the Master's degree. Many of these courses I had already taken in Prague, but I felt that it would be beneficial to me if I learned all I could about American forestry practices.

After all my classmates graduated that year, I stayed at the school, working during the summer and taking some courses offered during the summer. During that school year Marian finished her requirements for a Bachelor degree and a teacher's certificate, and her sister Helen completed hers as well. All three of us graduated in June 1952 in the Centennial Class of Duke University (1852-1952).After graduation, Helen entered graduate school, and in January, Marian's parents left to serve in the Methodist Church in Vienna, Austria.

The job situation was not particularly bright during the year of my graduation. What I was looking for was a career with a private forest industry, rather than state or federal forestry. I accepted a temporary position as a research assistant on the Duke Forest, a fairly large forest which the School managed as a research facility in support of the various studies conducted by the staff and graduate students. My assignment was to complete all the new maps for the forest. That was my primary job, occasionally interrupted by some field work, working with different graduate students.

The most noteworthy event during my time as a research assistant took place during the fall after my graduation. The University received a gift of a parcel of forest land from the Duke Power Company of North Carolina. The property was located some 30 miles south of Durham, near a little town of Pittsboro, and lay on the bank of the Haw River. The tract of timber measured about 300 acres. I was given the job of surveying and marking the boundaries of the property.

Since I needed an extra man to help with the job, I asked some of the graduate students if they would be interested in the work and in earning a little pocket money. Ralph Griffin, a PhD candidate volunteered for the job.

In a couple of days we surveyed the boundary lines, set the corners, and cleared the property lines of brush. The only thing left was to mark the boundaries with paint. After we got back to the school, I looked for some paint, buckets and brushes in the work shed. There I saw a backpack spray gun. It occurred to me that this would be a faster way to mark the trees: just put the paint in the canister, put some air in it, and presto, you spray the paint on the trees. It would save a lot of work, I thought.

The next day, early in the morning Ralph and I put a gallon of blue boundary paint in the canister, attached the hose with a nozzle to it, got in the truck, and headed out of town. The plan was to stop at the last filling station in the little town of Bynum to put the air in the canister.

At the filling station, I got out of the truck, grabbed the canister, and knelt down by the air compressor next to the only gas pump in the station. Ralph was leaning against the gas pump and looking at what I was doing. I attached the air compressor hose to the air valve on the canister, letting the air in.

While this was going on, a brand spanking new black Studebaker sedan rolled up to the pump. No sooner had the car stopped at the pump, when the nozzle at the end of the hose blew off, and the hose began whipping wildly from side to side, spraying the side of the Studebaker, the gas pump, and Ralph, who was leaning against the pump. Luckily the windows of the Studebaker were all closed, so that at least the interior of the car was spared the color scheme change-over. Apparently I had put too much air into the canister, which caused the nozzle to come off. The whole thing was over in just a few seconds.

The lady driver got out of the Studebaker looking stunned, unable to say anything, tears coming down in buckets. Finally, after a few seconds, she asked, "What am I going to do now? I just bought this car about ten minutes ago in Pittsboro. What now?"

I was lucky that the paint did not reach me, except that my hands got some paint on them as I struggled to subdue the hose gone amok. I did not even want to look at Ralph; he looked like some kind of blue alien from another planet.

I went to the lady and told her, "I am awfully sorry, Ma'am, but don't you worry about anything. You just take the car back to the dealer before the paint dries. I am sure that they will be able to clean up the car for you." I realized that I was telling her all this without really knowing who was going to pay for all of this.

"We are from Duke University," I continued talking to the stricken lady, "and I am sure that their insurance will pay whatever it takes to get your car cleaned up. I'm terribly sorry for your big inconvenience. Can we do anything else to help you?"

By then the station owner was out surveying the blue wonderland and laughing. I apologized to him also for the mess we had made of his station, but he said not to worry about it, he'd get it cleaned up. Then I went into the store and called Mr. Blackman, my supervisor at the Duke Forest and told him what had happened.

Laughing, he said, "You did the right thing. Our insurance will cover the damages. Just come on back and get cleaned up."

By that time Ralph had managed to get most of the paint from his face and hands, and wiped off at least the worst of the paint from his clothes. Needless to say, we did not paint those boundaries that day. That had to wait a couple more days before we got back to finish the job with a paint bucket and brush. Then as we passed by the filling station we could still see the blue paint all over the pavement around the gas pump.

Not too long after that episode, the Director of the Duke Forest told me that Union Bag and Paper Corporation, a pulp and paper company located in Savannah, Georgia, was planning to establish a forestry research department and was looking to hire foresters interested in such work. Of course I was interested, but I felt that they were probably looking for people with an advanced degree, such as a PhD. It looked to me like a once-in-a lifetime opportunity, but what chance did I have against all the highly qualified applicants?

I prayed about it, I talked to Marian, telling her that it might be a waste of time. But she responded, "Go for it, you never know...."

So I put in my application. It felt like tossing a bottle in the ocean. When the recruiter came to the campus, I showed up at my appointed time, and then the first question came. "Do you always wear that beard?"

"No, "I said, "Usually I have no beard, but the town of Durham is celebrating a bicentennial, and the Chamber of Commerce asked all male citizens to grow beards and wear period attire as a part of the celebration. So I'm just trying to go with the flow...."

That seemed to satisfy his curiosity, and he proceeded to ask his programmed questions.

"Thank you for coming to see me, and thanks for your interest in our company. You will hear from us in a couple of weeks or so."

We shook hands, he left, and I found myself on pins and needles for the next two weeks. Time seemed to stand still for those weeks. Finally a letter came, with the corporate logo of Union Bag and Paper Corporation in the upper left hand corner. I tore open the envelope and unfolded the letter:

"Dear Mr. Malac, we are pleased to offer you a position as a research forester with our company...."

When I read this wonderful news, I felt guilty, and asked God to forgive my lack of faith. Thanks to God's amazing grace, yet another door had been opened for me.

I was invited to come to Savannah to meet with the personnel people and my future boss, William Wesley Johnson, to sign all the necessary papers and to set the date for the start of my professional career. Even the name "Wesley" had the unmistakable imprint of God's hand on my life. We were to move to Savannah in late May, and I was to report for work on June 1, 1953.

In May of 1953, the president of Duke University was having an open house on the occasion of moving into a new residence on campus. Marian and I were invited to see the beautiful new house and to meet with some of the friends we had made. When we spoke to the president's wife as she met us at the door, we mentioned to her that I had just gotten a job with Union Bag and Paper Company in Savannah, Georgia.

"Oh, I envy you! Savannah is just the most beautiful city in the South," she gushed. "I just love Savannah!"

"Thank you," I said. "I hope we'll be happy there. The most important thing is that I got the job."

I did not want to tell her that I was not nearly as enchanted with Savannah as she seemed to be. I remembered our first impression some months before when we drove through Savannah to Brunswick to visit my former classmate who worked there for Brunswick Pulp and Paper Company. The trip on the old coastal highway, US 17, took us straight through some of the slummiest part of Savannah. At that time we both said that it would be the last place where we would want to live. But later when I went to Savannah for my job interview, which happened to fall on St. Patrick's Day, I saw the other side of Savannah's face. The azaleas were in full bloom, the beautiful Savannah park squares were full of spring blooms, and the Spanish moss draped the ancient live oaks lining the street. So perhaps the president's wife was not too overly generous with her praise of Savannah.

Chapter
18
Welcome to Savannah

The last week in May 1953 we left Durham with a rented U-Haul trailer loaded with all our possessions and headed south for Savannah, Georgia. It was a long, hard drive, especially down the old US 17 highway, the only main road leading into Savannah from the north. Not being used to pulling a trailer, I found the trip slow and tiring. The weather was hot and the traffic heavy. Finally, after almost ten hours of driving we reached Port Wentworth, a Savannah suburb and major seaport. We stopped at a motel for the night to rest up after the long trip.

At that time, Savannah was a typical southern port city with many different industries. The population had a generous mixture of ethnic groups, including the Irish, Scottish, Greek and German nationalities, and a large number of African Americans. Apparently, the depression years had left the city age-worn and rundown. The editor of the local newspaper had called Savannah "the beautiful lady with a dirty face."

However, in the late fifties the local Historical Society launched a huge effort to salvage and   preserve the inherent beauty of Savannah. Through those efforts the city later became one of the most attractive southern cities on the East coast. Practically the entire downtown section is now on the National Register of Historical Areas.

The morning after our arrival, we drove into Savannah and started looking for possible places to stay. We found several places advertised in the local newspaper and made a few phone calls from the downtown post office. Not having any luck in finding an apartment, we drove back to the motel. There I discovered that my billfold was gone. I remembered that I had taken the billfold out of my pocket when making the phone calls, and laid it on the shelf below the phone. Evidently I forgot to pick it up after I made the call, I thought. We drove back to the post office to look for the billfold, but it was not there anymore. Someone had already picked it up. My social Security card and my Duke University ID card, and my driver's license were gone, as well as about a hundred dollars I had in cash. We knew that we would not see that money again.

Almost a year later, though, we received a letter about my missing billfold. A Savannah man had found it in the post office, and seeing the Duke ID card tried to find me or my address there. Since we had already left the university without a leaving a forwarding address, he kept on searching and eventually located our Savannah address. We recovered all my documents including all my money. He was just another of God's angels.

After I lost my billfold, I went to my new employer, explained our predicament, and asked for an advance on my salary. Not only did I get an advance, but also received a lead on temporary housing for us. After a few days' stay in a room in a private home, we found a small bungalow for rent in Garden City next to a new house the owner had built for himself. It was located closer to my place of work.

As was our custom, after finding a place to live, we started to look for a church family. For several Sundays we visited the large Wesley Memorial Methodist Church downtown, quite far away. But then we discovered the small neighborhood Methodist Church close by in Garden City. There we found a warm welcome, joined the choir, and soon we became active members of our new church family.

It was there in Garden City that our extended family experienced its first loss. God called home Marian's mother, Marian D. Bartak. She was then living in Vienna, Austria with her husband, Dr. Joseph P. Bartak, serving in the Methodist Church there. Marian was especially sad because we were already expecting our first child. Her mother already knew about

141

the upcoming blessed event, and had been looking forward to seeing her first grandchild. The loving comfort and support of our new church family eased our pain and provided spiritual help in our time of need.

Early the next year we bought our first house. It was a three bedroom bungalow located in the fairly new Highland Park subdivision in the southern part of Savannah. We moved there in January, and along with the new house we found a new church home as well. It was a small neighborhood church on 53rd and Bull Street with about 350 members. We joined the choir, the Sunday School, and immersed ourselves in the life of the church, making new friends along the way.

With my good job and becoming settled in our new home, we finally felt that we were ready to raise our family. After all, that was a reason we had come to America, a place to raise our children in a Christian environment with unlimited opportunities for education and the pursuit of individual happiness.

The first to arrive was our son, Roy David, in March 1954. Our second child came in November 1955, Deborah Ruth. Both were healthy and vigorous. Even before the children were born we had agreed that Marian would stay home with the children at least until they reached school age. We knew that this would cause some financial hardship, but we felt strongly that it was the best for our children. We knew that God would bless our decision. Looking back on those sometimes financially stressful years, we now see clearly God's hand in all of these experiences and rejoice in His blessings.

Several years later we learned that Marian's father was ready to retire and return to the U.S. from Vienna, and would like to come live with us, but he would need a room of his own. That meant that we would need a larger house. With Marian's part time teaching and my having had several raises in my salary, and with Marian's father's help, it seemed we could afford a larger house.

In 1958 we had a new ranch style house built in Paradise Park still farther south, off White Bluff Road. The house had four bedrooms, a screened back porch and a carport with utility room, and a small yard. Marian's father moved in with us that same year. Later I enlarged and enclosed the back porch into a den with a corner fireplace.

In March 1960 our third child, Timothy Alan was born. All of us, and especially the children, enjoyed having their grandfather around. I only wished that our children could have had the opportunity to meet my parents as well. By this time I had not seen my parents for over ten years. For me, it appeared to be an unreachable dream, given the circumstances.

Then an opportunity arose that I thought might give me a chance to see my parents. My company allowed me to go to Vienna, Austria, to attend the world conference of the Forest Research Organizations held in 1961. I wrote to my parents about the upcoming trip to Vienna, and suggested that perhaps they might be allowed to make a trip to Vienna, where we could meet in the church that my father had once served. But their request was denied. I did, however, make the trip, and visited the house in Vienna where I had been born, met our neighbor, who was still living next door to our former parsonage. He invited me to visit the church where both my father and Marian's father had served. There were still several members there who remembered me as a little child. It was a bittersweet, but joyful experience.

In 1964 Marian's father became seriously ill and ended up in the hospital, where he spent about five months, bedridden and in constant pain. In September he was moved to the newly opened Magnolia Manor, a Methodist retirement center and nursing home in Americus, Georgia. After only a month there, he passed away on September 30. When we received an emergency phone call from there, we were able to make it to

Americus, but by the time we arrived he was already in a coma. Marian was able to hold his hand until the last few moments. We were there when God, whom he had served so diligently, called him home.

Several times we had asked my parents if it would be possible for them to come visit us in America, but always the answer was no. The communist government would not allow anyone to travel to the Western countries, especially if they had relatives who had left the country illegally. Only after my father had retired, did the government finally allow them to visit us, when we provided funds for their trip. It was not easy for them to secure the necessary travel documents, as my brother-in-law told me years later. It required knowing certain people, dropping a few names, greasing a few palms here and there, and interminable hours of waiting in line.

In the early spring of 1966, my mother and father came to visit us. We left the children with an elderly couple from our church and drove to New York, so we could meet my parents at Kennedy Airport. We stayed overnight with Marian's sister Helen's family, who then lived on Long Island. The next morning at the international arrivals terminal we waited anxiously for my parents, seventeen long years since I had last seen them. A lot had happened during those years: the escape, arriving in America, the hard beginning in Texas, graduation from college, getting a job, the children, a promotion to manager, and the memories of my childhood, all came flooding in as we stood there waiting for my parents.

When my mother finally came through the door into the waiting area, she stood there for a moment looking at me as if she could not believe that I was standing there, with my arms outstretched towards her. Then as she realized that I was there in body and flesh, she ran into my arms. We embraced, not believing and not wanting to let go. We looked at each other with tears of joy filling our eyes, and embraced again, unable to utter a word. Finally we let go of each other and said how glad we were to see each other. Then I embraced my father, who waited patiently for his chance to see his prodigal son. It was an emotional and joyous occasion. Praise God for His goodness and mercy. Then Marian had her chance to greet my parents as well. At the baggage claim we gathered all of their luggage and went out to the parking lot. We loaded everything and everybody into our station wagon and headed south toward Savannah.

My parents stayed with us for almost three months. They enjoyed the children, even though they had difficulty communicating with them. My father knew a little English. The children learned a few words in Czech, like "thank you" and "please," and got along quite well with sign language. Tim was in kindergarten at the time, but he was home sick with the mumps one week while they were there.

At our church, my parents became the center of attention. At that time I was directing the church choir as a volunteer, and my father helped by singing in the choir. He had a beautiful tenor voice. Once or twice my father and I sang a duet as special music. The church honored our family that year as the "Family of the Year."

Even this blessed time had to come to an end. Though we invited my parents to stay as long as possible, they needed to go back home. My sister's second child had been born a few months before my parents left for America, and my sister would have to go back to work soon and would need my mother's help. This time we were able to arrange for them to leave from Savannah to New York to catch their overseas flight. The airlines provided the necessary escort for them, to help them make airplane changes in Atlanta and in New York. I am so grateful to God for allowing us to see my parents again after such a long separation. It became even more precious to me now, because that was the last time I saw my father alive. Once again we were by ourselves with our children. We cherished the memories of the years and days that we had with our parents and our children's grandparents.

I tried to spend as much time with our children as I could, but my job took me away, often for days at a time, so most of my time with them was on weekends. During school vacations we would take extended camping trips, visiting exciting places in many beautiful National Parks. We tried to show the children some of this wonderful country, to see not just the natural beauty, but also the rich history of this great land. I also worked with the Boy Scout troop at our church, especially when Roy became a Boy Scout.

Many of our camping trips took us through Texas, which I considered my "home state" in America. There we would visit with Uncle Charlie and Aunt Martha on their farm. Uncle Charlie had the ideal fishing creek for the kids there. The creek did not look very impressive, it looked more like a deep gully, but at the bottom of the gully ran a stream of cool clear water, and in that water were lots of blue catfish. You could just walk along the bank of the creek and see the large schools of catfish huddled in little pools of crystal clear water, stacked up fin to fin like cars in a parking lot. But they were finicky eaters; they would not bite on anything but the local big fat grasshoppers. Needless to say, every time we stopped by Uncle Charlie's place, we caught a mess of blue catfish that Aunt Martha would fry up for dinner.

The lion's share of responsibility for bringing up our three children fell on Marian's shoulders. And I thank God for Marian's perseverance and dedication in her job as mother. She instilled in our children the love of God, and the importance of living a life of service to others. Her influence as a Christian mother and teacher helped our children to achieve an amazing success in high school as well as in college, and later in their respective careers. Our sons are engineering graduates of Georgia Tech and working for private industry. Our daughter is a graduate of Furman University and the University of Virginia, and is serving in the public sector as an officer in the U.S. State Department Foreign Service.

All three of them are happily married and between them have eight wonderful children, our grandchildren, which are a source of great joy to us. They are also involved in the church life of their respective church congregations, and are involved in their community as well. Good American citizens all! How did we ever deserve such rich blessings? We can never thank our Heavenly Father enough for His guidance, strength, and power and grace that helped us overcome so many obstacles in our lives.

In 1972 my father passed away in Pilsen, but we did not know about his passing until about a month later when we received the obituary notice by mail. At the time I was on one of my out-of-town business trips in Franklin, Virginia, when Marian called me on the phone in my motel room to tell me the sad news. I said a prayer of thanks for my father, but felt so detached from the event, not having been there, that it was almost like reading a newspaper obituary of a stranger. It just was not the same as being there with him at his passing with the rest of the family, celebrating his life and sharing in the grieving. My father was 82 years old when he died.

Some time later some good news arrived in a letter from my sister. She wrote that the government had declared a general amnesty for many of the political prisoners and especially for the people who had left Czechoslovakia for political reasons. Now there was an opportunity for us to visit my homeland. Marian right away suggested that I should go and visit my family, some of whom I had not seen for 25 long years.

"If I go, we'll all go!" I said. "Roy is at Georgia Tech, Debbie is at Furman. That leaves only you, Tim and me. If we wait until summertime, Tim can go with us. Roy and Debbie plan to have summer jobs here in Savannah and can home-sit for us."

Chapter
19
Back to the Homeland

Late in 1973 we began to plan our trip to Czechoslovakia for the next spring. It was still a communist country, and there was a lot of red tape to overcome. We had read newspaper reports about expatriates who went back but found themselves in trouble when trying to return to America. Some were even arrested just before they were to leave. To avoid any problems we decided to go strictly "by the book."

I called the Czechoslovak Embassy in Washington, D.C. to inquire about getting a visa to Czechoslovakia. A pleasant voice asked:

"What is the purpose of your visit?"

"I left Czechoslovakia in 1949 without a passport," I answered, "and I am now living in the United States. My parents are still living in Czechoslovakia and my wife and I would like to visit them and my other relatives."

Upon hearing that, the pleasant voice disappeared and became quite grumpy, and very officious. The official began to ask all sorts of personal questions about why I left, where I had crossed the border, how much money I was making, and so on.

"I believe that is really none of your business," I answered. "All I want to know is how I can get a visitor's visa."

"If you'll not give us this information, you cannot get the visa.," he snapped back. "Even though you are living in the U.S., you are still a citizen of Czechoslovakia." Then, his voice suddenly becoming more pleasant and accommodating, he suggested: "If you send us a check for $1000 we will be happy to cancel your Czech citizenship and you can get your visa."

"No thank you," I replied. "You just keep the citizenship and I will keep my thousand dollars," and I hung up the phone.

After that little incident, we decided to book our entire three week trip through a local travel agent who took care of making all the necessary arrangements, including getting the visas with no questions asked.

Our trip took us to Paris, where we spent a couple of days enjoying the sights and the food. Then we traveled by train to Munich, Germany, where we rented a car for the last leg of our trip. After spending time in Munich, we traveled to Erding, some twenty-five miles east of Munich. I hoped to visit the former German Airbase, now an American Airbase, where I had spent the last two years of the war as a forced laborer. But unfortunately, I was not allowed to get on the base.

We continued on our way, stopping for a little while at Regensburg, at the new bridge over the Danube River, the place where I had caught a ride with a Russian military convoy as I made my way home from Stalag Erding at the close of World War II.

Approaching the Czech border, I grew more and more apprehensive about returning to Czechoslovakia. We stopped at the last little German village to stretch our legs, and to buy gasoline and a few snacks before continuing to the border. As we were leaving the quaint village, a little black cat darted across the road just ahead of our car.

"Oh, no, look," Marian said jokingly, pointing at the cat. "You know what they say. Bad luck! Maybe we should turn around and go back."

"Why," Tim and I laughed, "it's just a little cat like any other cat, black or not. We've gone this far, we're going in!"

Soon we reached the German side of the border. When the guard there saw our American passports, he just waived us on with a smile. In just a couple of minutes the Czech border station came into view. The place looked deserted, the barrier was down blocking the road. I stopped the car and waited for someone to show up. Finally after about a half hour the barrier was raised and we could drive through. We stopped in front of the station, where a young guard, fully armed, came to the car, took our passports and disappeared into the building. A short while later, he came back and said that it would take a while to get clearance.

As it turned out, it took over an hour, with the guard standing by the car all the while. As we waited, I looked at the countryside ahead of us. There was a high chain link fence with barbed wire coil on top, and inside the fence was an area about fifty feet wide cleared of all vegetation, to afford a clear view of the border. About a hundred yards to my left was one of the towers guarding the border. I could imagine the armed border guards scanning the borders with their binoculars and with machine guns at the ready.

I surprised our young guard when I started talking to him in Czech. While Marian kept punching me in the ribs to be quiet, I told him that I had left Czechoslovakia about 25 years before and that I crossed the border not far from here, and that I now lived in America. He asked how I liked America, and what it's like to live there.

Finally an officer emerged from the station and asked us to come with him. We all got out of the car and followed him into the station.

"What is the purpose of your visit?" asked the officer.

I told him that we planned to visit my parents, my sister and brother, and do some sightseeing. Then he asked how long we intended to stay. When we told him that we planned to stay for two weeks, he said that right away we had to exchange a minimum of $14 per person per day of our stay for Czech crowns. And we were to provide them the itinerary of our trip, who we planned to visit and the places and hotels where we would stay.

After we finished with all the paperwork, the officer came out with us to the car to check all of our luggage in the trunk of the car. We had to open all the suitcases, and he went through them, asking all sorts of questions about the contents.

"And don't forget" he added, "that you must report your presence to the local police within twenty-four hours in each place. Your sister had already called us, asking if you had arrived. She and her husband were waiting for you in the next village outside the border zone, but since you did not show up by noon, they left for home."

By that time it was about 2 o'clock in the afternoon. While all this was taking place, only one other car with Czech license plates had passed through the border checkpoint. Obviously, there was not much traffic coming through in either direction.

When we finally got underway, we were struck by the desolation of the surrounding countryside. We saw abandoned farmhouses, neglected fields, villages and small towns looking drab and rundown. Nothing looked like I remembered it from my youth, when the little villages were bright and colorful, full of flowers, fields were lush and green, full of promise of a bountiful harvest. In those days people had been smiling, laughing, singing while they worked in the fields and meadows, and greeting each other as they passed by. What a stark contrast this was!

Now the few people we saw were in old shabby clothes, their faces full of fear and suffering, shuffling along the road, looking down. One could almost feel the weight of their suffering on their shoulders. It reminded me of the ghostly scenes we had seen in pictures of the Russian gulags and the German concentration camps. The gray, overcast skies over the countryside added a surreal and poignant backdrop to the scenes of utter despair and hopelessness.

We drove on in silence for most of the two hour drive from the border to Pilsen. Even that large city of almost a quarter million inhabitants had the look of a ghost town. Shell-pocked houses, dirty streets, a few ancient cars, buses and streetcars, and the same feel of hopelessness on people's faces. Everywhere there were communist party flags with the hammer and sickle, huge banners and posters extolling the blessings of the "worker's paradise" and the "glory of the great and glorious communist party and the new social order," along with pictures of the "liberators", the Russians. It was sickening to us.

Since we did not know exactly where my sister lived, we decided to drive to the main railroad station in downtown Pilsen and phone my sister. We reached the railroad station about four o'clock on Thursday afternoon of the first week of our planned two week stay. We found a telephone inside the railroad station and called my sister, who told us to wait there, that they would meet us there in about fifteen minutes. We stood outside the station on the sidewalk to wait for them.

Those were anxious minutes for me. Marian and I had not seen my sister for over 25 years, and had never met her husband. What would she look like? Would I recognize her? And what about her husband? Would he be glad to see us?

Soon we saw a large, somewhat well-worn Russian "Volga" sedan pull up by the sidewalk. A tall man got out, then my sister, and their two small children, a boy and girl. Yes, that was my sister alright, still as pretty as I remembered her. She was a bit older, with a few wrinkles on her face, but with perfectly coifed hair, which was always her pride and joy. We rushed into each other's arms, said nothing, just let the tears flow. After a while we stepped apart and looked at each other at arms length, enjoying each other's tear-stained faces.

My sister Jirina introduced us to her husband Gusta and their children, Libor and Marcela. Our son Tim handled the introduction well, even though he did not speak Czech. Having made all the introductions, my sister suggested that we all go home where we could talk in private. Our rented shiny little red Volkswagen was attracting quite a few onlookers by now. I did not really understand at that moment my sister's reluctance to talk to us in public. Only later, in the safety of their home, did we find out that it was not safe to fraternize with strangers in public, especially those who looked unmistakably like Westerners.

At home, my mother was waiting for us. It was a joyful reunion, marred only by the sad fact that my father was no longer with us, having passed away only a few years after my parents had visited us in 1966.

Their house was truly a do-it-yourself family project. Gusta, with the help of Jirina, my parents, and my brother had built the house. It was a comfortable house with a basement partially used as a garage, plus a story and a half. It was all masonry, with a yet unfinished brick exterior, and it stood in a small fenced yard with a locked gate. After an enjoyable time visiting and eating an evening meal, we headed back to town to our hotel on the main square.

Chapter

20

Life in the "Worker's Paradise"

On Friday morning Gusta met us at our hotel to take us to the police station where we had to register our arrival in Pilsen, as required by law. We had the uncomfortable feeling of being watched all the time but never welcomed. Strangers in the homeland!

The rest of the day we spent at home with my mother and sister and her family, catching up on all those years we had not seen each other. I was especially struck by how much the political situation had affected their personal lives. I felt guilty and ashamed, thinking of all the freedom and the abundant life I had enjoyed over the past twenty-five years in America, compared to the bleak and hopeless existence not just of my sister and her family, but of all the people in this beautiful country that had once been my home as well.

The next day Gusta drove us and my sister to visit Marian's cousin Martha in Carlsbad a premier spa and resort town just about an hour away. My mother stayed home with the children. We enjoyed visiting with Martha and her husband, talking about the good old days. After lunch we walked the world-famous promenades of the spa, "taking the waters" and enjoying the beautiful surroundings. Then it was back to Pilsen and to our hotel to rest up.

On Sunday we went to church with my mother. The beautiful church with the parsonage where I had spent eight years as a young boy was still there. But it had been taken away from the Methodist Church by the communist government and turned into the lecture hall of an engineering school. What was left of the congregation was meeting down the street in one of the small rooms of a Hussite church. When my father left this Methodist church in 1936 to serve the church in Slany, the congregation counted over a thousand members, but the congregation we saw that Sunday morning consisted of only nine old people, including my mother. The minister was a retired Salvation Army officer. Needless to say, I was moved to tears. But the spirit of the Lord was present in the service. We were greeted privately by the minister as visitors from America, but we were not allowed to speak officially to the congregation. One of the old ladies present was a seamstress who used to sew all our clothes when we were children. She still remembered me, and we shared a few lovely memories and shed a few tears.

For the next few days we enjoyed the hospitality of my sister's home. We made visits to Gusta's relatives, visited his brother's little cabin in the country, where they had a little garden. We toured the countryside, saw the ruins of an eleventh century castle Radyne outside Pilsen, and toured an eighteenth century palace, Kozel nearby. Surprisingly, we found this small palace better furnished with period pieces than the famous Versailles palace in France.

The next weekend we planned to be in Prague to visit with my brother Vlasta and his family, and to attend the Sunday worship service in the Central Methodist Church where we were married. On Friday morning we struck out for Prague. Gusta and Jirina with their two children drove their Volga and the three of us and my mother followed in our little red Bug.

Although we knew my brother's wife, also named Jirina, we had never met his four sons and their families. My brother Vlasta was living in one of the typically drab, socialist apartment houses in one of the suburbs of Prague. The apartment consisted of four small rooms, including a tiny kitchen, a miniscule bathroom and small entrance hallway. I could not imagine what it must have been like to raise four sons in this tiny space.

When the whole clan gathered for this impromptu family reunion, it was wall-to-wall people. We enjoyed the shared meal, the fellowship, and sharing life experiences over the last twenty-five years. Towards evening, Gusta and his family drove back home to Pilsen. Our mother spent the night in my brother's apartment, while we drove to a nearby high rise hotel Olympic that we had reserved through our travel agent.

The next day my brother Vlasta treated Tim and me to a first class tour of Prague. Marian was not feeling well and spent the day in the hotel resting and trying to get well. We saw most of the well known sights, including the centuries-old castle that was still the seat of government, the Old Town with its historic City Hall and the world famous clock, Wenceslas Square, and many other historic places.

On Sunday we all went to worship at the Central Methodist Church. That was an especially meaningful and emotional visit for both of us. This was where we both lived for a few short years, where we had met, where we worshiped, and attended MYF meetings. This was the place where I stole the first kiss from Marian, and it was the place where we were married 25 years before.

The worship service was lovely, but the attendance was small, and was held in a small room downstairs, not in the main sanctuary upstairs as we remembered. There were altogether about 25 people in the congregation, including Vlasta and our mother. Very few young people were there. Most of the worshipers were our age or older. Several people there still remembered us, especially Marian. Here too, we were greeted by the pastor and our presence was acknowledged, but we were not allowed to speak to the congregation. Only after the service did we get to speak with the people over tea, coffee and some refreshments. We enjoyed our visit, grateful to God for allowing us to be present at this sacred and for us, very special place.

Monday we drove out of town to visit the well known Karlstein Castle. We had been there before, but this time we found it quite empty, with none of the rare furnishings, nor the coronation jewelry we had seen there in the past.

Once again it was time to leave Prague and continue on our scheduled trip. We stopped by Vlasta's place to pick up my mother, who was to travel with us until we reached Uherske Hradiste in Southern Moravia, where she was going to visit with her sister for a few days.

Our first planned stop was Havlickuv Brod, where I spent my high school years. There I hoped to visit with some of my former classmates. We checked into our hotel, and then went for a walk. The hotel was located on the town square, only about three blocks from the high school. As we walked up the street toward the school, I happened to spot one of my classmates walking toward us. Even though I saw that he had recognized me, he just walked past me without acknowledging my presence. I was really stunned by the incident. Were people really that afraid to speak to foreigners?

Then I remembered Olga, a classmate, who as a student used to work part time at the local drug store. I decided to go there to see if by chance she might still be working there. When I walked into the pharmacy, there she was, standing behind the counter. She still looked the same as I remembered her.

I stepped up to the counter and started to speak, when she interrupted me, "Ahoy, Shaman, is it really you?" Shaman was my nickname; throughout the entire high school I was known as Shaman.

"It sure is," I said. "How good it is to see a friendly face."

Quickly she stepped out from behind the counter, took me by the hand, and pulled me into the back room, closing the door behind us.

She gave me a big hug and, as tears began to fill her eyes, she said, "Oh it is so good to see you here. But we can't really talk out here now. Can you come to my house this afternoon? I get off at 3 o'clock. I still live in the same "Glass Palace" where my folks used to live, and…"

"Wait a minute," I interrupted, "what's going on? I just saw one of our classmates on the street and he just ignored me. Why?"

Then she told me that it is not safe to talk with strangers, especially Westerners. There are communist informers everywhere just looking for someone to report on to the secret police." I could hardly believe what I was hearing.

"I'll call all the classmates that I can reach, and we'll set a time for us to meet tonight in someone's home where we can talk without being afraid," said Olga. "Are you by yourself?"

"No," I answered, "my wife and our youngest son Tim are with me."

"That's just great," Olga gushed, "bring them with you. We'll all be glad to meet them." I gave Olga the name of our hotel, and she promised to call to let us know when and where we should meet that night.

It was a wonderful gathering that evening. About a dozen of my former classmates came, some even from out of town fifteen or twenty miles away. Behind closed doors, in the relative safety, we shared our life experiences since we left school. Some of us had gone to Nazi labor camps, others had stayed at home. They shared their incredible stories of lives behind the Iron Curtain: of the persecution, the political condition, the loss of freedom. The entire country was plunged into the dark ages. But despite the difficulties, their spirits were alive, full of hope and faith in a better future eventually. We sang together, accompanied by a guitar, some of the country songs we used to sing as teens, songs sung around campfires, and songs from America. When we left, we promised to keep in touch, and I promised to come to the next class reunion if at all possible. One of my classmates even asked me to come and stay overnight at his house, since our room at the hotel had only three single beds, and with my mother and Tim there were four of us.

The next day we left for Moravia. On the way we stopped briefly in nearby Jihlava at our old parsonage, to visit with the pastor there, whom we had known as a college student in the youth group in Prague.

We traveled on to Herspice, arriving there about noon. We stopped for a short visit with my Uncle Pavel, my father's youngest brother. We were greeted with a bowl of freshly picked sweet strawberries, cookies and tea. Pavel had just been released about a week before from the state penitentiary where he had been for violation of some farm policies. My uncle was a very outspoken critic of the communist regime and had been fined and jailed several times for speaking out against the communist government.

His youngest daughter, Nadya, had escaped from Czechoslovakia along with her husband and their three young boys during the Dubcek regime in the late sixties. Dubcek had tried to loosen the strict Stalinist form of communism and establish an independent rule of communism with a "human face." Needless to say, the Soviets did not like his approach, and Dubcek was deposed and imprisoned within a year. It was during that brief period of the "Prague Spring" that people were allowed to travel outside the country into some other   countries of the Soviet block. Hundreds of people used this opportunity to leave the country never to return. Nadya and family left for a vacation in Yugoslavia but then applied for asylum in Austria. They spent some time in an Austrian refugee camp before they were able to come to America. The American Lutheran Church sponsored them and hundreds of such refugees, bringing them to America and helping them to be resettled.

After we left my Uncle Pavel, we headed to Uherske Hradiste to visit with the Hanak family, my aunt and uncle. My aunt was my mother's oldest sister Helena. We checked into a pension according to our pre-approved itinerary and went to a family reunion given by my cousin Bozena, my aunt's oldest daughter. Bozena put on quite a feast. She was a medical doctor, her husband was some sort of business man. Her youngest brother Jan, an architect was living in Slovakia. I mentioned to my uncle Hanak that we were to drive to Slovakia the next day and would like to stop by to see my cousin Jan. He called Jan on the phone to let him know about our intention.

After he hung up the phone he told us: "Jan said that it's not a good idea. Since he works for the State as a public official, he cannot afford to be seen with anyone from America." By now I should not have been surprised by my cousin's response, but I was really dumbfounded. After all, we're family, I thought.

"Jan suggested that he'll drive over tonight," my uncle continued, "and we can visit here where nobody else can see us. He lives only about 25 or 30 miles from here, so it won't take long for him to get here." I did not want to appear too inflexible, so I agreed to that. About an hour later Jan came in. Right away he apologized to me and tried to explain the situation.

"I'll spend the night here at my sister's," he said, "and in the morning, my dad and I will drive my car and you follow us. When we get to my town, I'll take you by my house and point the house out to you, but we'll not stop. We'll drive on out of town into the woods, and there we can say our goodbyes. That's the safest way to do it. Again, I'm sorry about this, but that's the way it is nowadays." There was not much I could say after that. I felt sorry for Jan and all the family. This was the celebrated "worker's paradise"?

I could not sleep that night. My God, what's happened to this once beautiful, free country? What's happened to these people? "All things work together for good to them that love God," I recalled the scripture verse hanging on the wall in our kitchen. Do I really believe that?

Early next morning we said our goodbyes, got in the car and followed Jan's sedan. My mother did not go on with us, she would spend a few days with her sister and then return to Pilsen by train. We drove on through the beautiful countryside and soon reached the outskirts of the little town where Jan lived with his family. In the middle of the town we slowed down, and as we approached a block of apartment houses, Jan's father stuck his arm out of the window and pointed up to the second story of a gray building. That was where Jan lived.

We speeded up again, heading east out of town and into the countryside. Soon we reached some wooded area and then turned off the main highway onto a gravel road. We drove for about a half mile into the woods and stopped at a small clearing. Jan pulled off to the side of the road, stopped the car and got out. I pulled behind him. His father also got out of the car and all three of us got out of our car too. Jan was looking around as though to make sure nobody was watching. We embraced, said goodbye, and we got in the car and drove away, not looking back.

"That was some kind of weird," said Tim.

"You're right. Very strange! Just remember this," I told him. "I hope you'll appreciate what we have in America."

Once we got back on the highway, we turned northward and headed for the Tatra Mountains in northern Slovakia. For two days we toured the beautiful Tatra Mountains, the quaint villages, the beautiful countryside, and also enjoyed the wonderful traditional food in the local eateries.

Then we turned southward and headed for the capital city of Slovakia, Bratislava. We spent about half a day sightseeing there and then drove on toward the Austrian border. Having experienced the protracted passport inspection on the Czech border, we were not looking forward to a repeat performance. But to our surprise, when the Slovak officer saw our American passports, he just smiled, waived us on, and wished us a safe journey. That was a surprise!

Our next stop was Beautiful Vienna, the "Paris of the East." We checked into a nice Pension, freshened up, and went sightseeing. The first place we headed for was our old parsonage in Huttledorf. Our neighbor, Mr. Vrba was no longer living next door to the parsonage. He had passed away shortly after I visited with him in the 1960's. But his daughter and her husband were living in the family house next door, and invited us in for some sumptious Viennese torte.

We toured the Schonbrun Palace and the beautiful gardens where our family had often gone for Sunday afternoon strolls. We rode the world famous "Riesenraad," the world's largest ferris wheel, where the gondolas are the size of a small railroad car and hold 20 to 25 people. And we toured other landmarks in Vienna. After spending a couple of wonderful days breathing the sweet air of freedom, we loaded up our little Bug and headed for a short tour of Salzburg before going on to Munich and our flight home.

After a long flight we arrived at New York JFK Airport. Our flight was late, so we missed our connecting flight to Atlanta and Savannah. The airline put us on a later flight that night, but it was diverted to Charleston, South Carolina, because of bad weather in Atlanta. We arrived in Charleston about 10 o'clock at night, but there were no flights to Savannah until the next morning. We told the airline we had been on the way almost 48 hours and asked for some way to reach Savannah before then. They finally offered to send us to Savannah by taxi. There was another couple going to Savannah who came on the same flight from New York. All five of us piled into the taxi van and were driven to Savannah.

We reached the Savannah airport after midnight. There we had the surprise of our life. Waiting for us with balloons, placards, and flowers was a group of people from our church to welcome us home. They had been waiting for hours. I believe that God's travel agents had been busy that day arranging that welcoming event. I can never forget such an outpouring of Christian love and care. We were simply overcome with joy after such a long and tiresome trip. How good it was to be back home!

After this initial contact with my family and friends in Czechoslovakia, God in His grace made it possible for us to go back about every other year until the year 2007. It was early that year that my sister Jirina passed away after a long battle with cancer. Only God knows if there will be another opportunity to visit there again.

Chapter

21

Life in Savannah

After such a triumphant return from our first visit to our former home, we began to feel more like true Savannians. We knew full well that Savannians just do not move to Savannah from another place. To be a real Savannian one had to have at least two or more generations of Savannah-born ancestors. But the folks were just so nice and friendly to us that they made us feel like real Savannians.

By this time we were heavily involved with our church work. After the Robert McIntire Methodist Church had lost its choir director, I volunteered to lead the choir until such a time we could find a qualified director. Well, I "volunteered" for almost eight and a half years. If it had not been for our excellent organist, I could not have done it. She helped when I got stuck on some difficult passages and picked up all the measures I dropped along the way. Although it was time-consuming, I enjoyed working with the choir and leading the congregational singing.

Besides the choir, I was teaching Sunday School, served on all sorts of committees, and was a member of the Administrative Board. It was during the time when I served on the Board that the church members decided to remodel the front of the church sanctuary by putting up a split chancel. The Board discussed the plans for almost two years without getting anywhere.

One of the charter church members, suffering from cancer, challenged the Board to get on with the job by offering a sizable amount of money to pay for the renovation. Even with that encouragement we were not making much progress. I decided to take the challenge head on.

My secretary at work told me that their congregation had just built a new church with a split chancel. I borrowed the blueprint from their church Board and used it to build a scale model of a split chancel sanctuary according to the dimensions of our church. I presented the model to our Board along with a rough estimate of the building materials and the time needed for the renovation. My plan was quite ambitious. I proposed that if our members would do the work, we could rebuild our chancel within one week without losing any worship time.

The Board approved the proposal unanimously. The next week we presented the plan to the congregation, which unanimously approved our plan, pledged their support, and set the date for the work.

To get a bit of a jump on the work, I started to build a new altar table about three weeks before the remodeling was to begin in the sanctuary. I worked in one room of the cottage that the church owned on the adjoining property. On the second weekend of my work on the altar table, a man walked in carrying with him a well-stocked tool box. I had never seen that man before.

"I hear you're planning to do some work on your sanctuary," said the man. "I thought maybe you wouldn't mind a little help."

"Oh, man! Come right in. I can use all the help I can get. Right now I am working on the altar table," I replied, showing him what I had done so far.

He jumped right in and started to work. I could see that he knew what he was doing. Even though he introduced himself, I no longer remember his name. Later I found out that he was a relative of one of our church members who told me that the man had never been to church in his life. But he was an excellent carpenter and cabinet maker. We finished the altar table in a couple of weekends.

In the meantime, one other member of the church had ordered all the lumber and hardware for the new chancel. The local lumber store gave us a break on the price and delivered the materials to the church free of charge.

Finally the startup Sunday came. We had a special service with the appropriate sermon, and a prayer of dedication. As soon as the last amen came, the entire congregation rolled up their sleeves and went to work moving furniture out of the sanctuary and tearing up the podium. The beautiful semi-circular altar rail built by one of the charter members was cut in two-foot sections that members bought as souvenirs, to be used at home as a worship center. By the end of the afternoon the entire front of the sanctuary was gutted down to the foundation.

On Monday morning we began the new construction. The men did most of the carpentry work, the ladies were cleaning, preparing lunches, and helping as gofers. After about two days of hectic work and long hours into the evenings, things began to take shape. The new altar rail was built in the social hall and the ladies were doing all the sanding, finishing and staining.

In the middle of the week, caught up in the spirit of rebuilding, the Methodist women's group decided to replace the carpet in the whole sanctuary. They raised the money, bought the carpet and had it installed.

There were people there working side by side that we had never seen in the church before. People showed up for an hour or two on their lunch break or after work. There were hardly ever fewer than twenty or twenty-five people working from early morning up to midnight.

Late Saturday evening we were putting on the finishing touches, cleaning up, painting, staining, polishing. Everywhere there was a wonderful spirit of cooperation, an almost holy fervor. We felt, as never before, the unity of spirit, the presence of the Holy Spirit. For all those who worked on this project, it became a Holy Ashram experience.

The next Sunday dawned in beautiful sunshine, the sanctuary shining bright, the new chancel full of beautiful flowers, beckoning the people to worship. At the dedication of the restored sanctuary, there was hardly a dry eye in the congregation. We were witnessing a miracle that God in His grace had performed in our midst. I'll never forget that special feeling of the presence of the Holy Spirit in that place.

By the mid-seventies we moved our church membership to the White Bluff Methodist Church in our neighborhood. This was a church started as a mission church about twelve years before. We had attended the inaugural service on Sunday along with Marian's father who was then living with us. Since that first service, we had moved into the Windsor Forest subdivision, so White Bluff became our neighborhood church. As usual, we joined a Sunday School Class, joined the choir, and became involved with the Methodist Men's and Methodist Women's organizations. Many of the members of our new church were old friends from Robert McIntire.

One Sunday afternoon, Father's Day, when Roy and Debbie were home from college, and Tim was out of school for the summer, they all decided to go to the beach with friends. Marian and I were working in the kitchen of our Windsor Forest home making blueberry jam when a storm came up with a lot of thunder and lightning. We had the stereo going in the den next to the kitchen, when an extra loud thunderclap caught our attention.

"It must have hit somewhere on the campus of Armstrong College," I told Marian. "It was very close." The Armstrong campus was just behind our back yard.

"That's right," she replied. "The lights flickered just now. You better go look into the back of the house."

"Well, the lights are on, the stereo is going. There's nothing going on," I said, trying to reassure her. But she insisted that she thought she smelled smoke, and looked into the garage, but saw nothing there. She kept insisting that I go look into the hallway by the bedrooms. When I reached the back hallway, there was a wall of thick, acrid smoke; I could not see anything. I ran back to the kitchen, yelling:

"Call the fire department and let's get out fast. The bedrooms are on fire." Marian dialed the operator and asked her to call the fire department. When we got out of the house, we could see the flames shooting up inside the windows of Tim's room. The fire engines arrived in minutes, and the firemen entered the house with their hoses. Soon people started gathering around, looking at the fire. The telephone operator evidently called the radio station, which started to broadcast news of the fire on the radio.

Our children heard about the fire on the car radio on their way back from the beach. My boss also heard the news at home and came out to see what he could do to help, as did many of our church friends. Even our insurance man came by and assured us that we would be taken care of.

Evidently the lightning had struck a power line on the Armstrong campus and traveled down the wires into our subdivision and into our house. Some neighbors reported their television and their air conditioning knocked out. Our electricity was on and the stereo kept playing until we cut it off, and someone quickly cut off the gas in back of the house.

Tim had a lot of electronic gear in his room, and apparently the power surge had started the blaze there. The firemen brought the fire under control fairly quickly, so that the worst damage was limited to his bedroom, the attic, and the hallway. The rest of the house mostly suffered smoke and dirty water damage. After the fire was out, we carried the furniture and belongings back into the garage. Roy, Debbie and Tim arrived in time to help with cleaning up some of the mess. They were invited to spend the night with some of their friends. Our church friends, Larry and Carol Tapp, who lived just a few doors down the street, invited us to stay with them for as long as it would take for us to find temporary lodging.

The next day the insurance adjuster came by to appraise the damage. It took several days to find a furnished apartment that we could pay for monthly, since most apartments were available only for long-term lease. We were told that rebuilding could take two to four months. With the help of a realtor we knew, we were able to move into a nearby apartment complex on a monthly basis after a few days.

Our house fire made the local newspaper. The article showed a picture of the damage, and the reporter who took the picture estimated the damage at around two thousand dollars. As it turned out, the rebuilding of the house interior took four months and cost about twenty-two thousand dollars. The walls and doors in half of the house had to be replaced. Tim had several musical instruments in his closet that had to be cleaned professionally and needed new cases, and he had to get new furniture and clothes. He also lost many of his model railroad items. Other pieces of furniture, paintings, dishes and clothing had to be cleaned. Even though we lost many valued and cherished items that could not be cleaned up, no one was hurt. With the help and support of our many friends, our church family, and by the grace of God we made it through unscathed, and praised God for His protection of our family.

Looking back across the thirty-five years we spent in Savannah, we have nothing but wonderful memories of this beautiful city and its hospitable people. We had some doubts about Savannah when we first learned that it would be our home. But as time went on, we began to see Savannah's good side. Savannah is truly a cosmopolitan town. It has much to offer its citizens. There is its rich history to recommend it: being founded by the English in 1733, its turbulent colonial times, the Revolutionary War for independence, the brutal Civil War, and then the depression era, all formed the character of Savannah.

Savannah also has a rich spiritual heritage. That is where the Wesley brothers, John and Charles met the Moravians who left their indelible mark on John Wesley's spiritual life. Savannah has many churches of all faiths, including the oldest Jewish Synagogue. I remember a statement made by a friend of mine, who served in the Merchant Marine during World War II. He said that every time one of their ships would dock in Savannah, looking at the many church spires, the crew would complain that there would not be much fun in this town.

Besides the religious and spiritual opportunities, Savannah offered a rich cultural experience. There was a wonderful symphony orchestra and an excellent Little Theater organization offering live performances of classic and contemporary plays. We became subscribers of both organizations. Marian and I sang with the Savannah Symphony Chorale, and I participated in the Little Theater.

I have always enjoyed the theater arts. As a young boy I took part in church plays that my father and mother put on in the churches they served. School plays were always a part of my education and enjoyment.

Savannah Little Theater was a nonprofit organization supported lavishly by the Jewish community, many of whom were prominent Savannah families. Of the 25 or 30 plays that I took part in, the three roles I most enjoyed were playing the father of Anne Frank in the "Diary of Anne Frank," Captain von Trapp in "The Sound of Music," and the lead role in "The Great Sebastian." All three of these plays recalled the days when Hitler's armies occupied most of Europe and enslaved millions of people. It was easy for me to capture the spirit of the resistance to the Nazi oppression by the characters in those three plays. In them I was reliving my own experiences with the forces of oppression, the nationalist fervor of the Nazis, as well as that of the communist regime later on.

During the latter years of our stay in Savannah, our daughter Debbie and son Tim joined me in several plays by the Little Theater, Debbie in acting, singing and dancing, and Tim in playing trombone in the small musical ensemble for some musical productions.

Another activity involving our family was scouting. When Roy reached the age of 12 we encouraged him to become a Boy Scout. Since there was no troop available close to our neighborhood, I asked our church to sponsor a Boy Scout troop, and offered my services as scoutmaster. Soon we had enough boys to form a troop and became accredited as a troop.

The highlights of these activities included our trip to the World Jamboree in Pennsylvania, and also a primitive camp in the mountains of North Georgia near Dahlonega. But by far the most adventurous trip I took our troop on was a floating trip down the Ogeechee River. We were vying for the 50-mile patch, which requires a fifty mile hike or canoe trip. The troop built two flat-bottom boats, each designed to carry a crew of eight.

We started building the boats early in the spring of the year. In June we finished the boats and took them for a trial run to the Ogeechee River. Everything went well with the trial, although the hardest part was learning to paddle in unison.

The next step was to select the starting point on the river, plan the trip including provisions, overnight stops along the river, and the final stop. Our trip started near Millen, Georgia, and ended at the mouth of the Ogeechee River at historic Fort McAllister. The total length of the trip was 75 miles and was to take seven days. Our flotilla consisted of two 14 foot john boats and two canoes.

Two days into the trip, one of the boats got caught in a swift current, the boys lost control of the boat, and the current smashed them into a submerged tree, puncturing the bottom of the boat. The crew managed to steer the boat onto a sandbar where we repaired the damage by taking a part of the decking in the prow of the boat and covering the hole by sandwiching it between two pieces of plywood decking.

The next day we had another emergency. Two of the boys who refused to wear their shirts got severely sunburned. We had to pull out of the river near a house and telephone the boys' parents to come take them home, because they required some medical help.

After that, the trip continued on without any further interruption. We completed the trip on Saturday morning, sunburned and tired, but proud of ourselves about our accomplishment. It was a historic moment. This was the first time that Fort McAllister was taken by waterborne forces. We spent the rest of the day at the Fort, which is a State Park, helping out with chores around the Fort.

Savannah was good to us. We enjoyed living there and making many good friends. We were happy to see Savannah emerging as one of the most beautiful Southern cities. Our sojourn in Savannah was the longest in our lives. We shall carry the memory of the "Lady with a Beautiful Face," Savannah, for as long as we shall live.

By the time we were preparing for our retirement, our family had grown with the marriage of our three children. The first to marry was our oldest, Roy. He and Carolyn Pierce were married in Savannah a year after Roy graduated from Georgia Tech. They had met at Brenau College in Gainesville, Georgia, where she was a student.

The second to take the marriage vows was our daughter Debbie, who met her future husband while on her first tour of duty as vice consul at the American Embassy in Cameroon, Africa. Her future husband Ron Olson was a colleague of hers at the Embassy. What I liked about Ron from the very beginning was that he wrote me a letter asking me for Debbie's hand in marriage. That reminded me of my "ordeal" of asking Marian's father for her hand. I knew what he had to go through and sympathized with him. We gave our daughter away in a lovely ceremony at the White Bluff United Methodist Church in Savannah.

The last to marry was our youngest son, Tim. He found his future wife, Theresa Brunn among the employees of the company he worked for in Melbourne, Florida. They were married in the First Methodist Church in Melbourne.

By the time we retired and moved to Blairsville, Marian and I had acquired two new lovely daughters and a handsome son. They have all become cherished members of our family and our pride and joy, along with our own children and also grandchildren.

Chapter
22

My Forestry Career

It's hard to remember exactly when or why I became interested in forestry, but already in elementary school I knew I wanted to be a forester. Forestry in Europe was always a very prestigious occupation. Especially in the small towns and villages, the most honored occupations were the doctor, the teacher, and the forester, in that order. After all, the foresters were privileged people. They had access to the king's forest, were the guardians of wildlife, and took care of the forests. Most forests there were the property of the nobility, the wealthy, the Church, the municipality or the state. Access to the forest by the general public was largely by special permit.

The forester was a rather romantic figure, very much a product of the European culture and folklore. Foresters wore fanciful uniforms and carried small ceremonial side arms. As the saying goes, girls liked a man in uniform. So it was small wonder that foresters appeared in many of the country folksongs, ballads and stories.

No matter that I had never actually met a forester in person, I just wanted to be one. My mother told me that one of her brothers was a forester, but I never got to know him. During World War I he contracted tuberculosis and died shortly after the war.

European forestry goes far back in history. Written records show forest management existed as far back as the fifteenth century. Many sons of the landed gentry and even of the royal and imperial families studied forestry. Generally the early forest management activities focused on game and wildlife management, to provide hunting opportunities for the forest landowners.   In modern times (the 19th century and later) management included more emphasis on the care of forest stands and forest products, as well as watershed management.

For those interested in forestry as a profession, special educational opportunities were available.   There were two-year schools for forest workers and technicians, four-year schools for supervisory personnel, and university level training leading to a professional degree in forest engineering.   In most European countries, forestry was, and still is, an engineering profession, and is offered by engineering colleges.

After merely dreaming of becoming a forester, my dream came true when I found myself a forester in America, working for a private pulp and paper company. To say that I was excited about my future would be an understatement. I was ready to go, to put in practice what I had learned in school in Europe and here in America.

I started as a research forester. Our Research Department at that time consisted only of three professionals: our boss Bill Johnson, Bob Erickson, and myself. Our workstation was a tract of forest land about 3600 acres in size in Effingham County, with one technician, Otis Seckinger, one army surplus Dodge four-wheel Power Wagon, and one mule.

Actually the mule belonged to Otis. Otis was a simple man, uncomplicated, hardworking, and generous to a fault.   He was a descendant of one of the original Salzburger families who came to Georgia with General Oglethorpe in 1733 in search of religious freedom. The Salzburgers settled in Savannah and later established their own colony in the neighboring Effingham County on the Savannah River.

Otis owned a family farm adjacent to our Experimental Forest. He knew every nook and cranny of those woods that he had hunted in since he was a young boy. During those early months of work Otis would invite me to come and "ride the woods" with him on weekends. He would let me ride his horse and he would ride his mule. He would tell me the histories of families that had settled this area. He told fascinating anecdotes about the local folklore, about the woods and animals. I will never forget the times I spent "riding the woods" with Otis. I am honored and priviledged to have known this unique man, a true American pioneer, and above all, my good friend.

There was no office building at that time. That was to be built later in the 1953-54 timeframe. Our operating budget was a whopping $27,000. Slowly I worked my way up, becoming Project Leader, and then the Assistant Manager.

Our Department grew, we acquired several more people, both professional and technician grade. After about 10 or 11 years, I felt the need to get more education about some specific areas of forest management. I inquired about the possibility of auditing some seminars at the different universities, but without much success. University studies required residence and work on a degree.

Finally I decided to enroll in the program at Duke University School of forestry leading to a Doctor of Forestry degree. My company generously agreed to pay me a half of my salary, to pay all tuition and board, and allowed me to take my company car with me. But after I finished the two required semesters of classroom study, and the development of my doctoral study project, I was asked by our Woodlands Manager to come back to Savannah to take over the Research Department as the Manager. Bill Johnson had decided to go back to school to work on his PhD degree.

Just like that, I became the Manager. Our Research Department had become known in the industry as one of the best private Forestry Research organizations. By then we had about 12 professionals and about the same number of technicians. The work was expanding, we were involved in a number of region-wide studies with a number of universities in the Southeast, and were making great progress in developing silvicultural treatment for improving the productivity of our forest lands.

We established satellite Research Stations in Virginia and in Alabama. We grew organizationally, requiring new positions, new people and new talent. We hired several PhD's to head up ever more demanding projects in forest fertilization, genetic improvement, soils management, harvesting, wood quality, growth and yield, and many more.

Eventually our department was given the responsibility to manage our entire woodlands inventory, harvest scheduling, and technical development. I became the Technical Director for the entire Woodlands Division, including all woodlands operations in all six southeastern states where the company owned forest lands.

As Technical Director, I became involved in numerous industry-wide committees dealing with air and water quality control, genetic improvement of southern pines, and national research priorities for the forest industry. It gave me a wonderful opportunity to visit and work with over fifty-plus Schools of Forestry across the United States, to work with the U.S. Forest Service Research Division, and with many State Forest organizations.

After 35 years of work in the Union-Camp Corporation family, I decided that the time had come for me to retire. I was 65 years old, and all three of our children had finished their education and had found their place in society as productive citizens. What else was there for me to do? Our Research Department now had over 40 fulltime employees, including six PhD's, our working budget was $2.5 million, and a capital budget of $2.0 million. I recommended my replacement to the management, and turned over my office to my successor.

My company gave me a big sendoff in a swanky country club on Skidaway Island, where I had the opportunity to share with my co-workers and friends my few minutes of glory.

I shared with them how God had led me from the Nazi jail cell in Erding, to this place at this time. In my wildest dreams I could not have imagined what God had in His will for me. Never would have I been able to achieve in my own country what I was privileged to do here in America. America took me in when I had no country and seemingly had no chance in the world. God gave me a wonderful wife to share my life with me, and gave us three exceptional children, whose accomplishments far exceed my own, and of whom I am unashamedly proud.

God gave me a priceless opportunity to be a part of the greatest adventure in forest management development that America has seen. The growth and development in the last 60 years of industrial forestry in America as a whole, and in the Southeast in particular, has no equal anywhere in the world. And I was privileged to be a small part of it. Think of it, I, one who came to America in 1949, a man without a country, with a wife and four suitcases, with eight dollars in my pocket being the sum total of all my possessions. Praise be to God for His unfailing grace and unmerited love!

EPILOG

In the autumn of our lives we are fortunate to live in a beautiful corner of our Father's great world. Blairsville is a peaceful little community, tucked away among the mountains of North Georgia. It was named at one time as one of the ten most desirable places for retirement in the United States.

In 1981 we bought a piece of woodland just south of Blairsville. It lies about halfway between the two highest peaks in Georgia, Brasstown Bald and Blood Mountain. We have a little over thirteen acres of beautiful rolling terrain, with several springs on them, and gorgeous vistas. For the first time in my life God has granted me my lifelong wish, to own and enjoy my own little piece of forest land. Where I came from, the ownership of forest lands was the right only of the nobility. To own a little piece of woodlands that I love above anything else is truly a blessing that I never dared to dream about. There are trees to enjoy, beautiful flowers, birds, butterflies, and deer, rabbits, possums and bears, all God's creation.

We started building our little retreat in 1986 and moved in after I retired in 1989. Now I am employed as a keeper of a thirteen acre estate, while Marian is the CEO and administrator and the financial officer of this enterprise. I am not sure how Marian feels about her job, but I am in seventh heaven.

Soon after we moved to our new house in Blairsville, I received a phone call from Dr. Brown at the School of Forestry at the University of Georgia in Athens telling me that I had been elected by my peers in the State of Georgia into the Georgia Foresters Hall of Fame. It came as a shock to me because I had never expected anything like that. It was humbling to me and at the same time extremely exciting. There is no greater honor in a professional career than to be recognized by one's peers. They surprised me with a great banquet held here at the State Conference Center at Unicoi State Park. What a wonderful ending to an exciting and satisfying career.

We are a part of a wonderful church, the First United Methodist Church of Union County. We sing in the choir and I occasionally teach Sunday School to our peers, and we are involved in many other activities of the church.

I have found a new hobby – playing a mountain dulcimer. It's a simple three-stringed instrument. It offers an opportunity to play anything from simple folk songs and ballads to classical music of such greats as Bach, Mozart, and others. It produces an intimate, soothing sound that, I imagine, is of a heavenly genre.

For several years I volunteered in the local Middle School grading math and science papers and tests of seventh and eighth graders. I also take out meals once a week to the shut-ins across the county, as one of the many volunteers of the local Meals on Wheels service.

We have traveled across the U.S., Canada, and Mexico with tours sponsored by the Society of American Foresters, we traveled to Europe, visiting our relatives in Czech Republic, on to Thailand, Asia and Senegal, Africa, visiting our daughter who has served in various positions with the U.S. Foreign Service.

God has blessed us with eight lovely grandchildren, and as of this writing, our first great-grandchild, a happy little girl. We enjoy our visits with our children and their families. We are proud of their accomplishments, and thank God that they, too, are finding their places in His service.

I have already outlived my father; my mother lived to age 90. Marian has outlived both her parents. We do not know what God holds in store for us, but of one thing we are very sure and that is that God is with us. Thanks be to God for my life full of miracles!